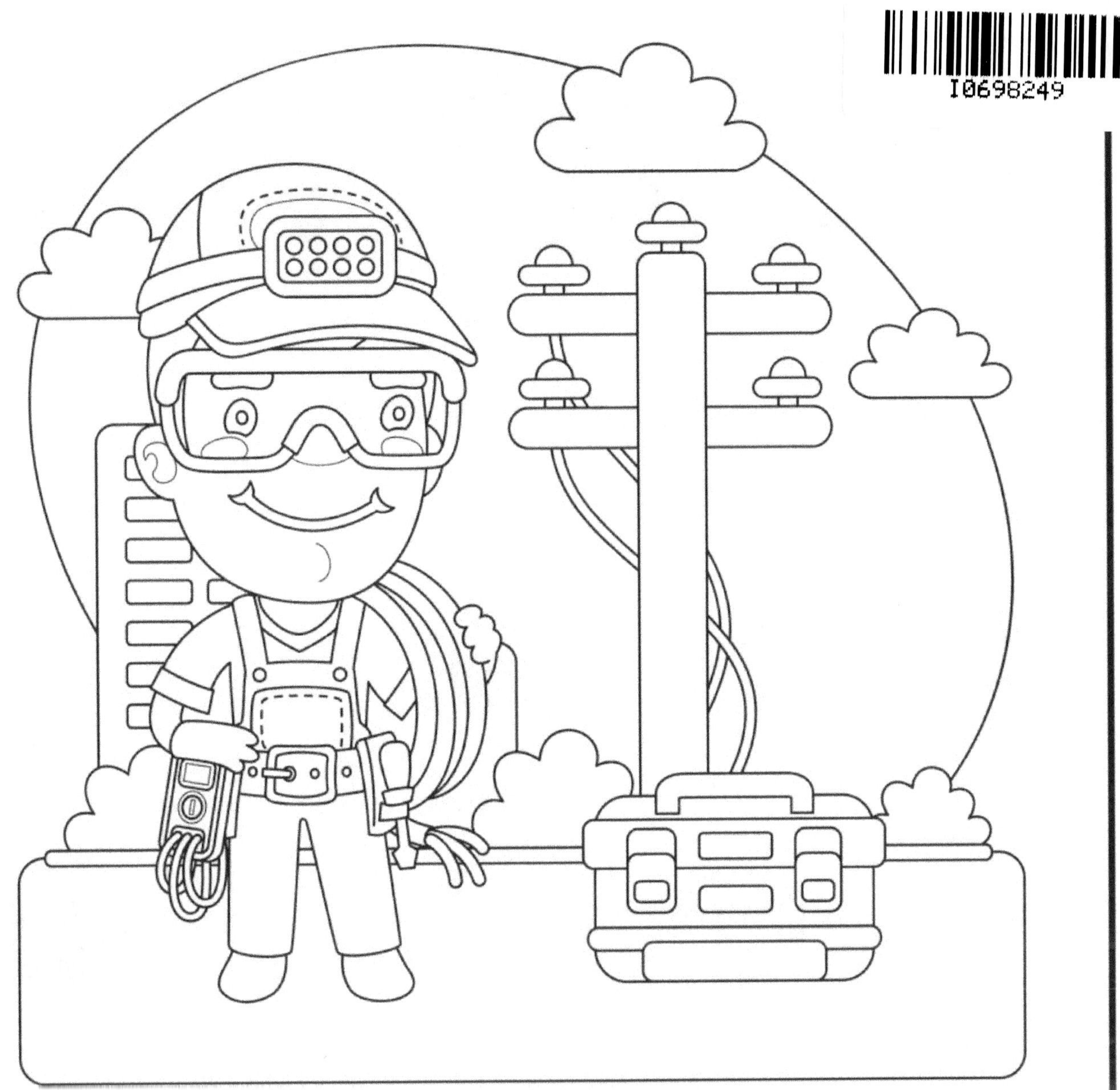

This Book Belongs To

COLOR TEST

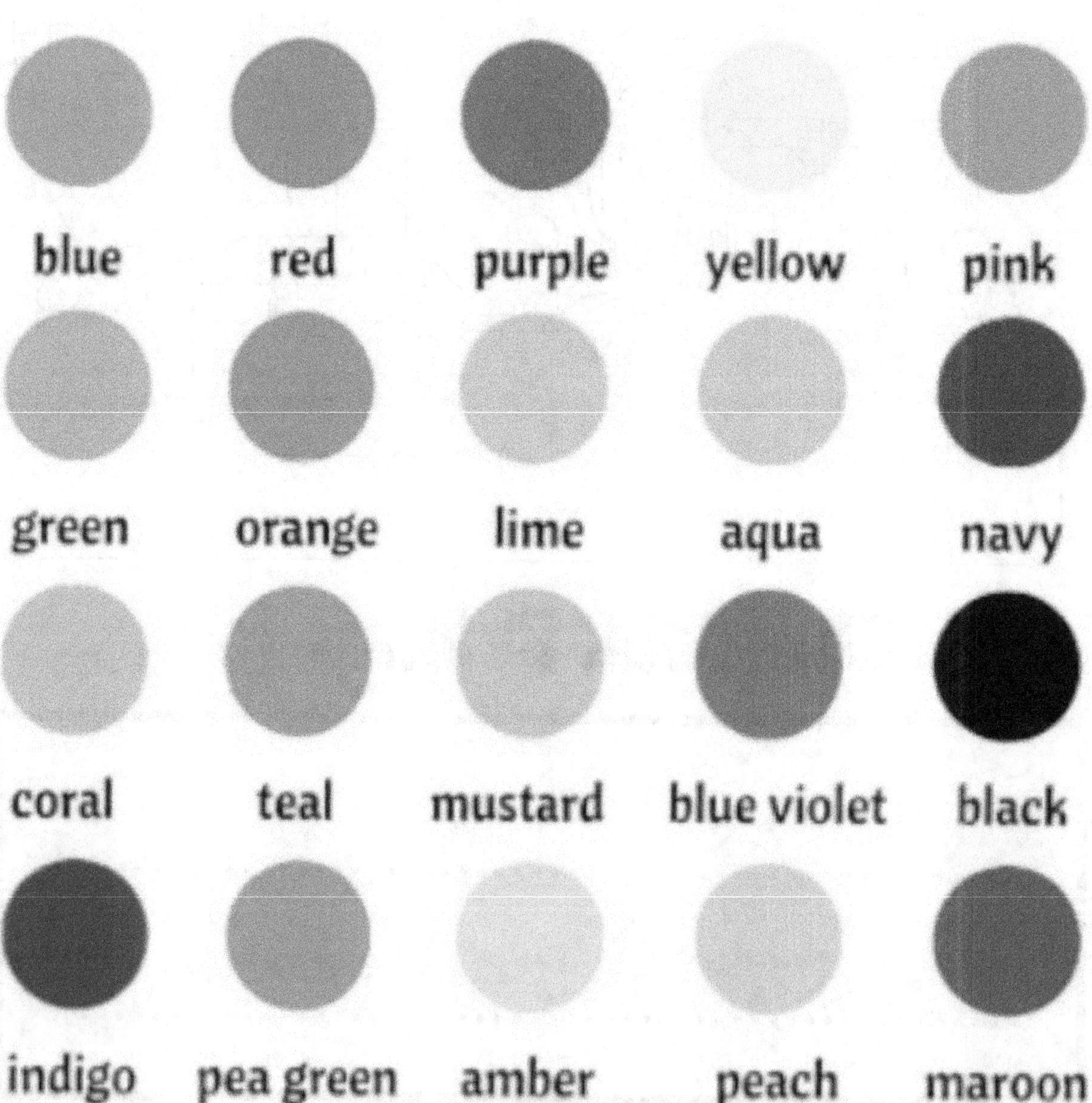

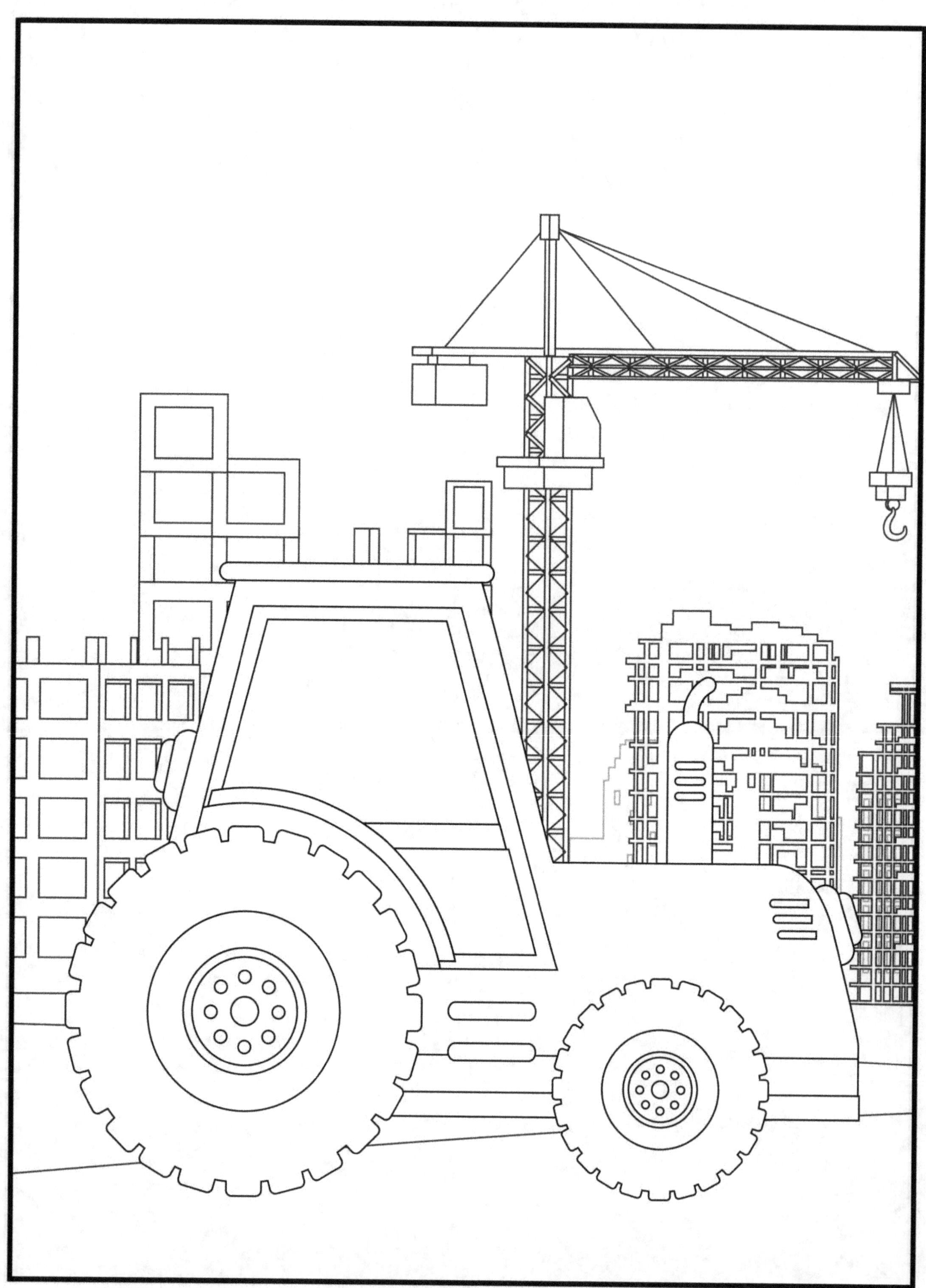

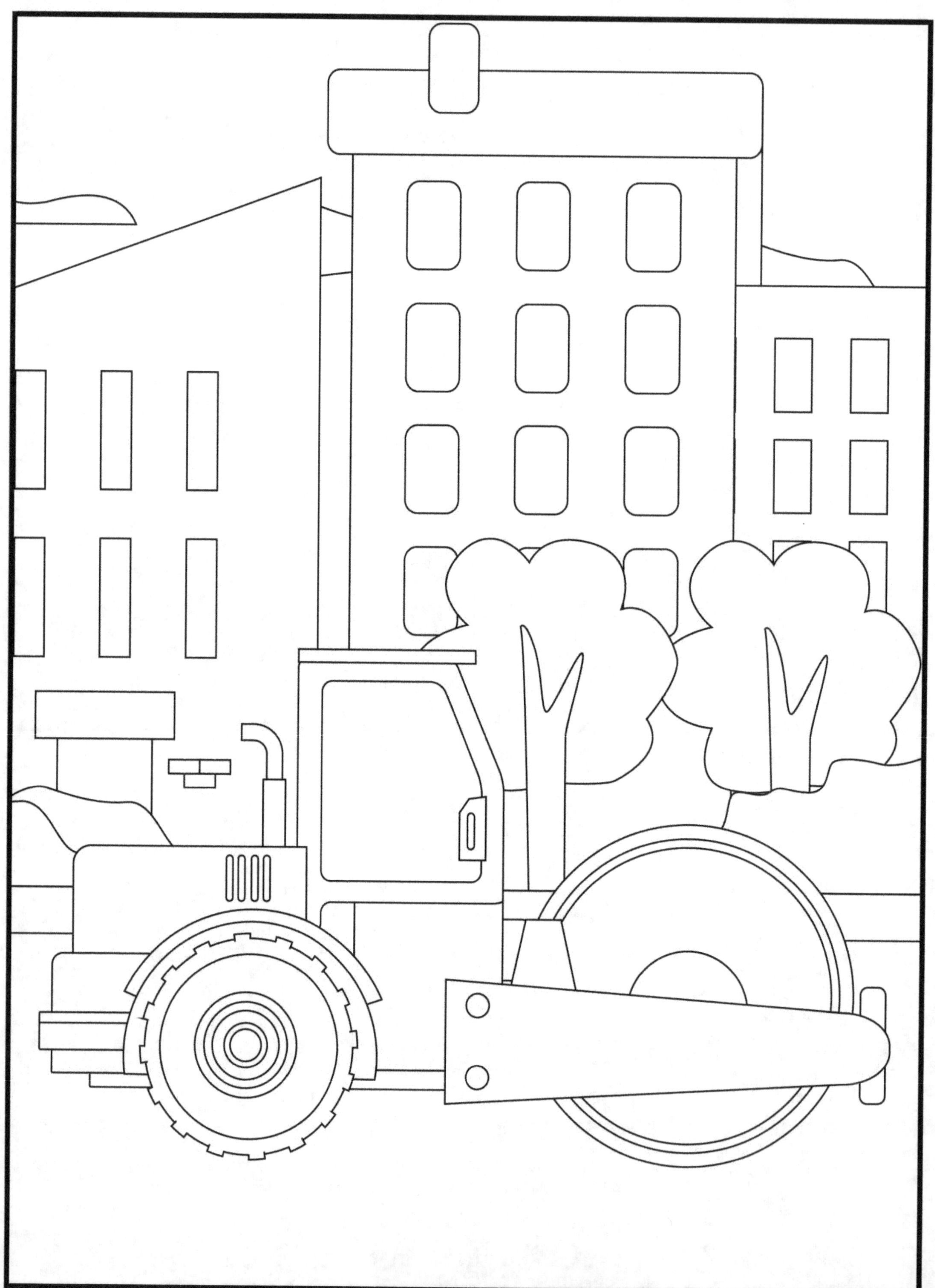

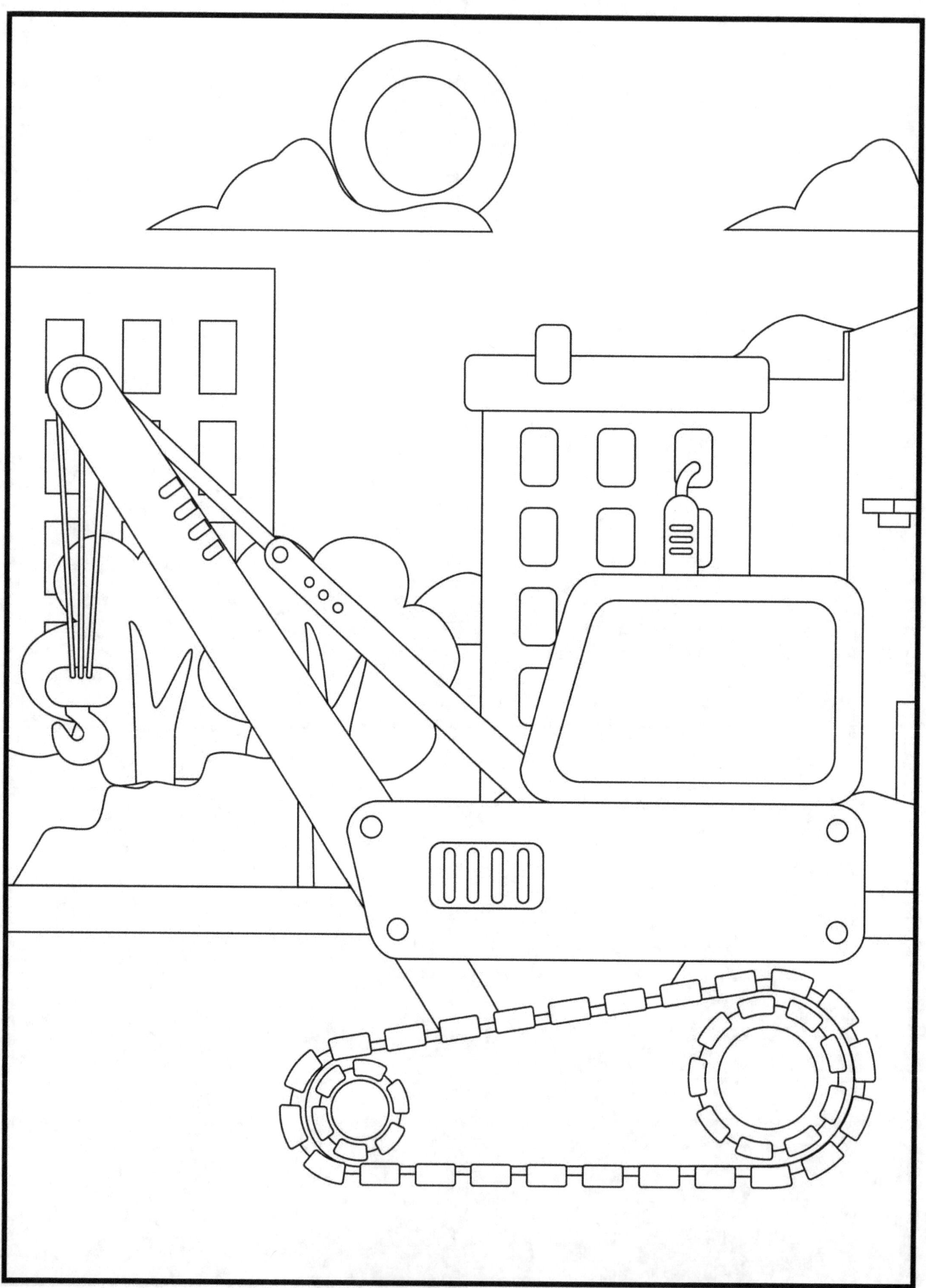

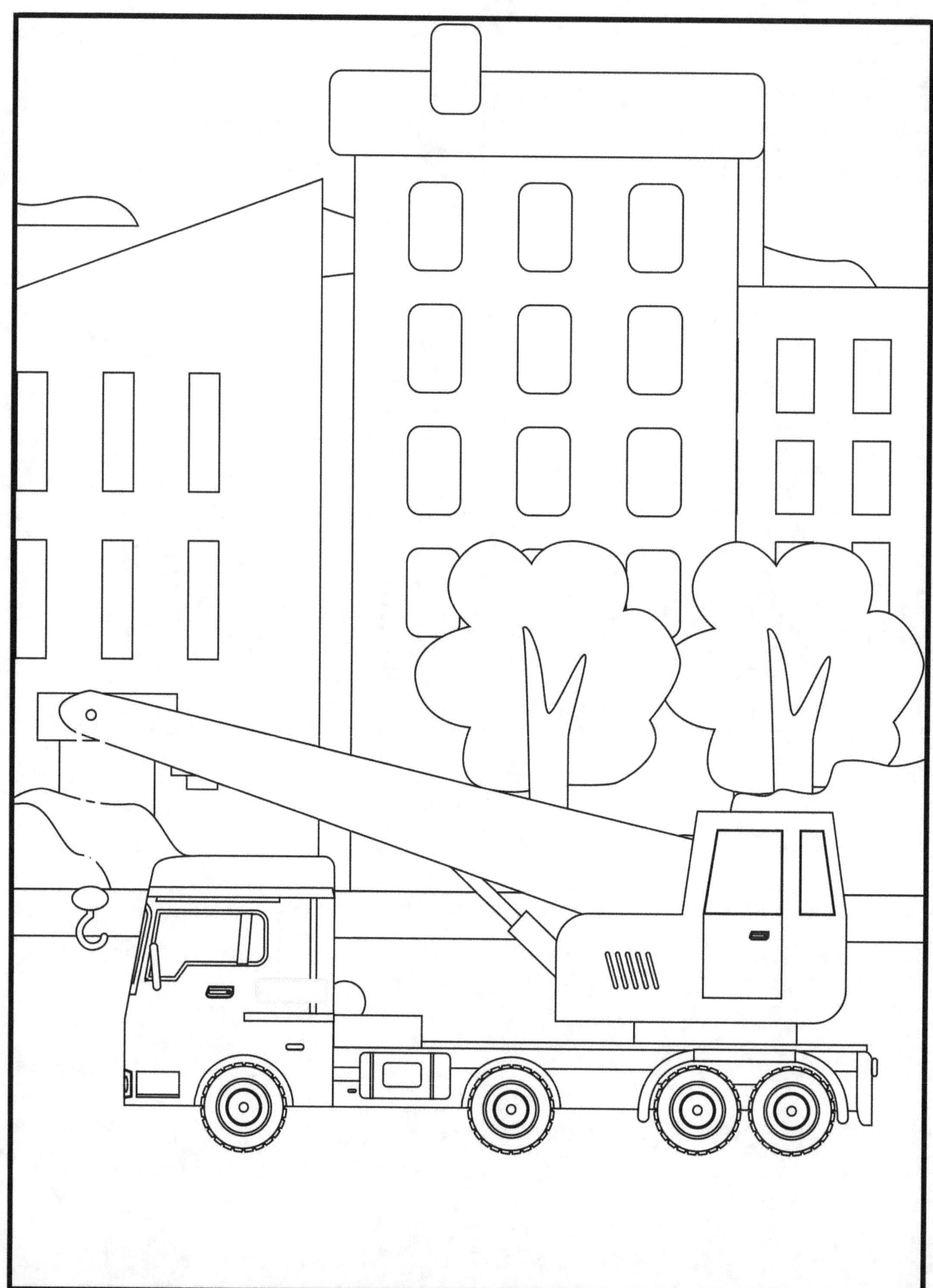

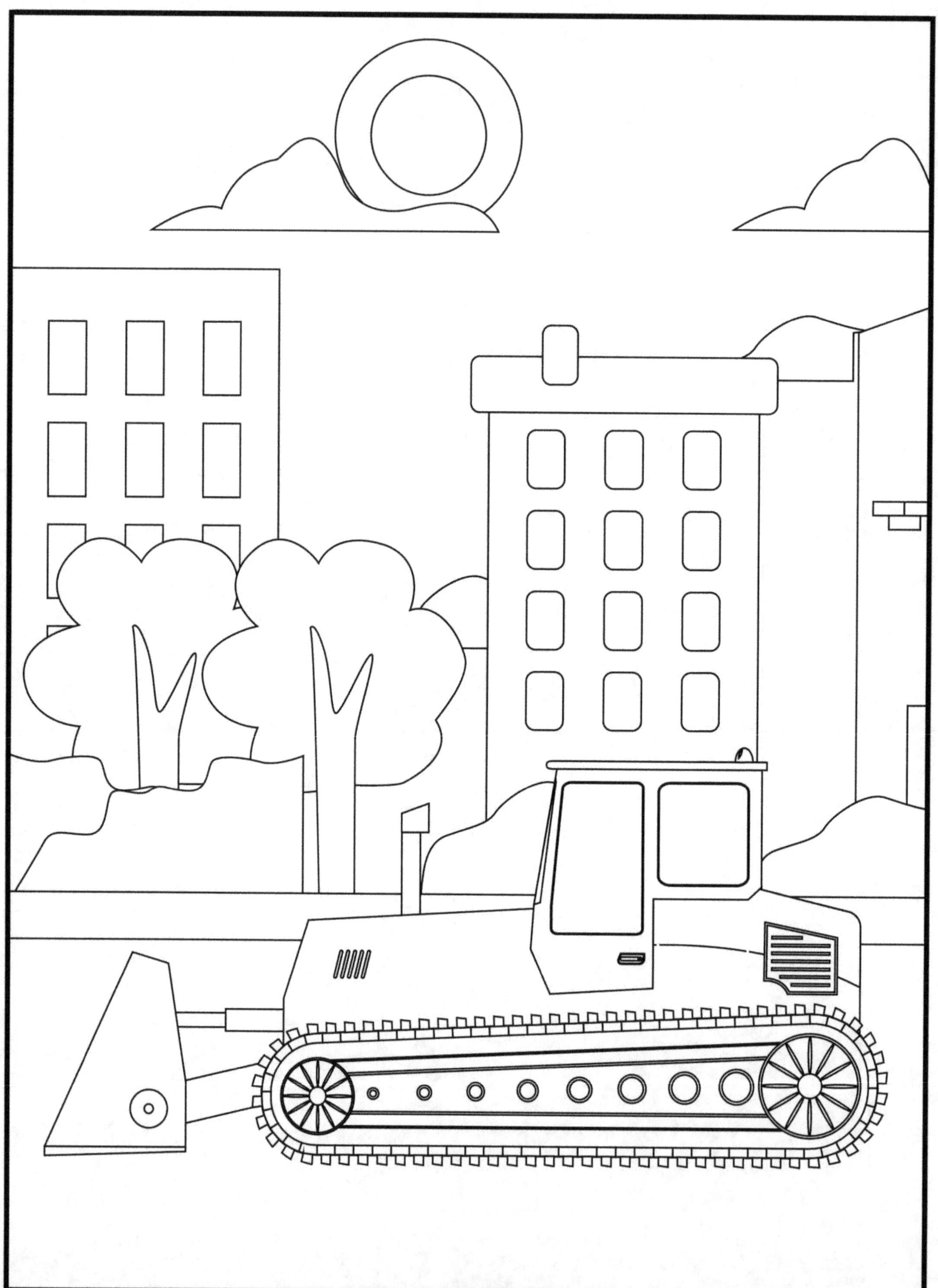

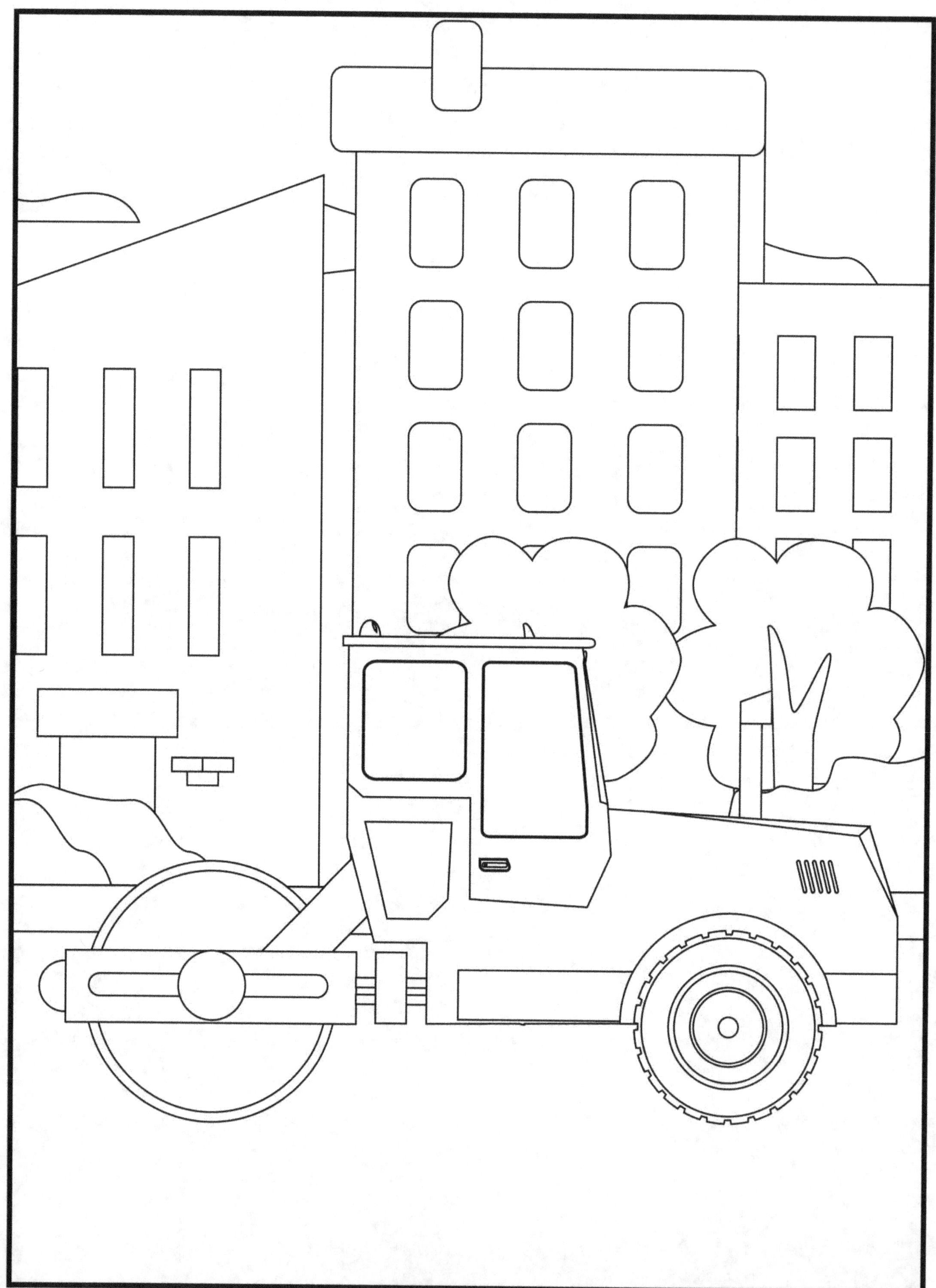

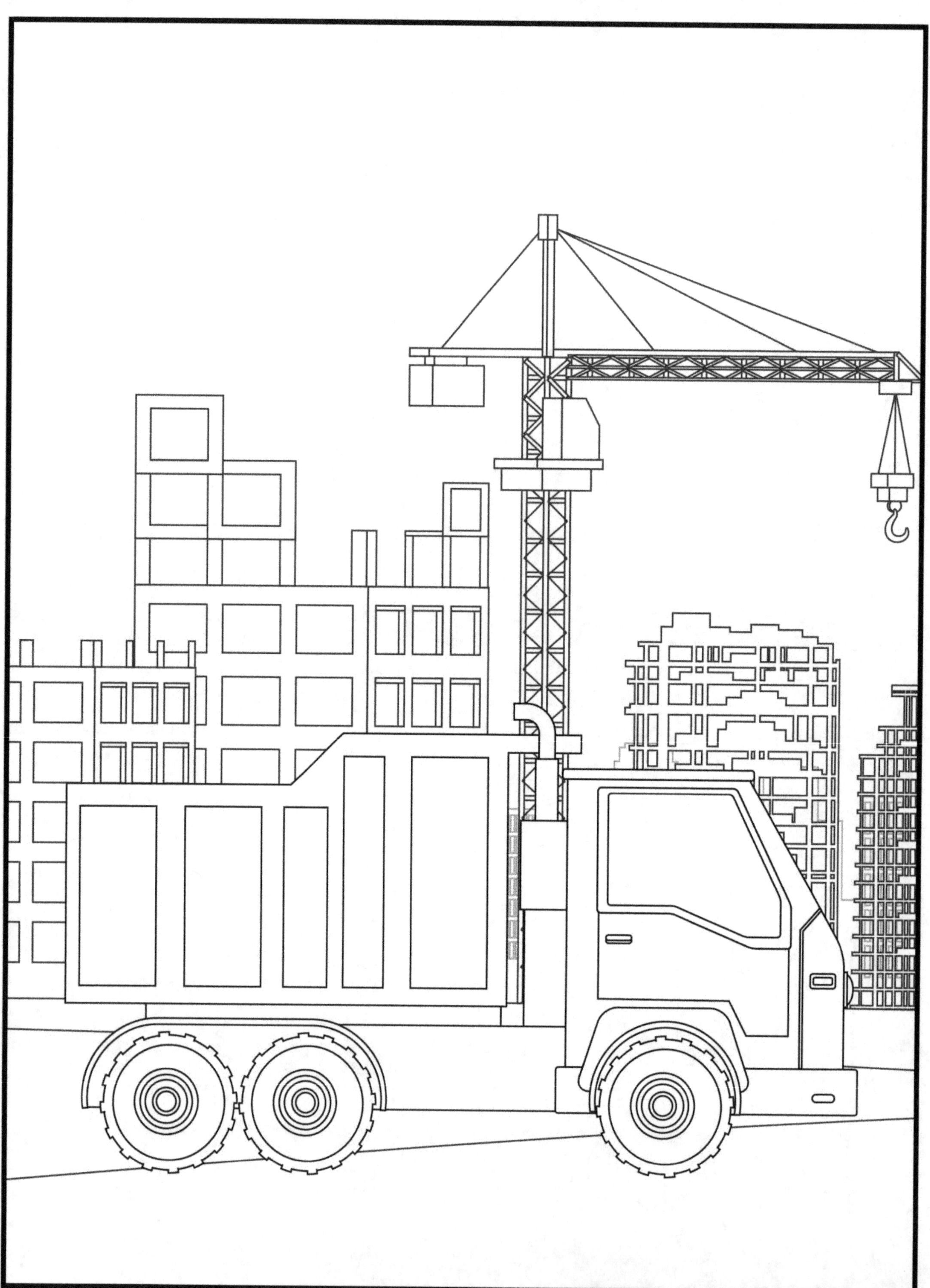

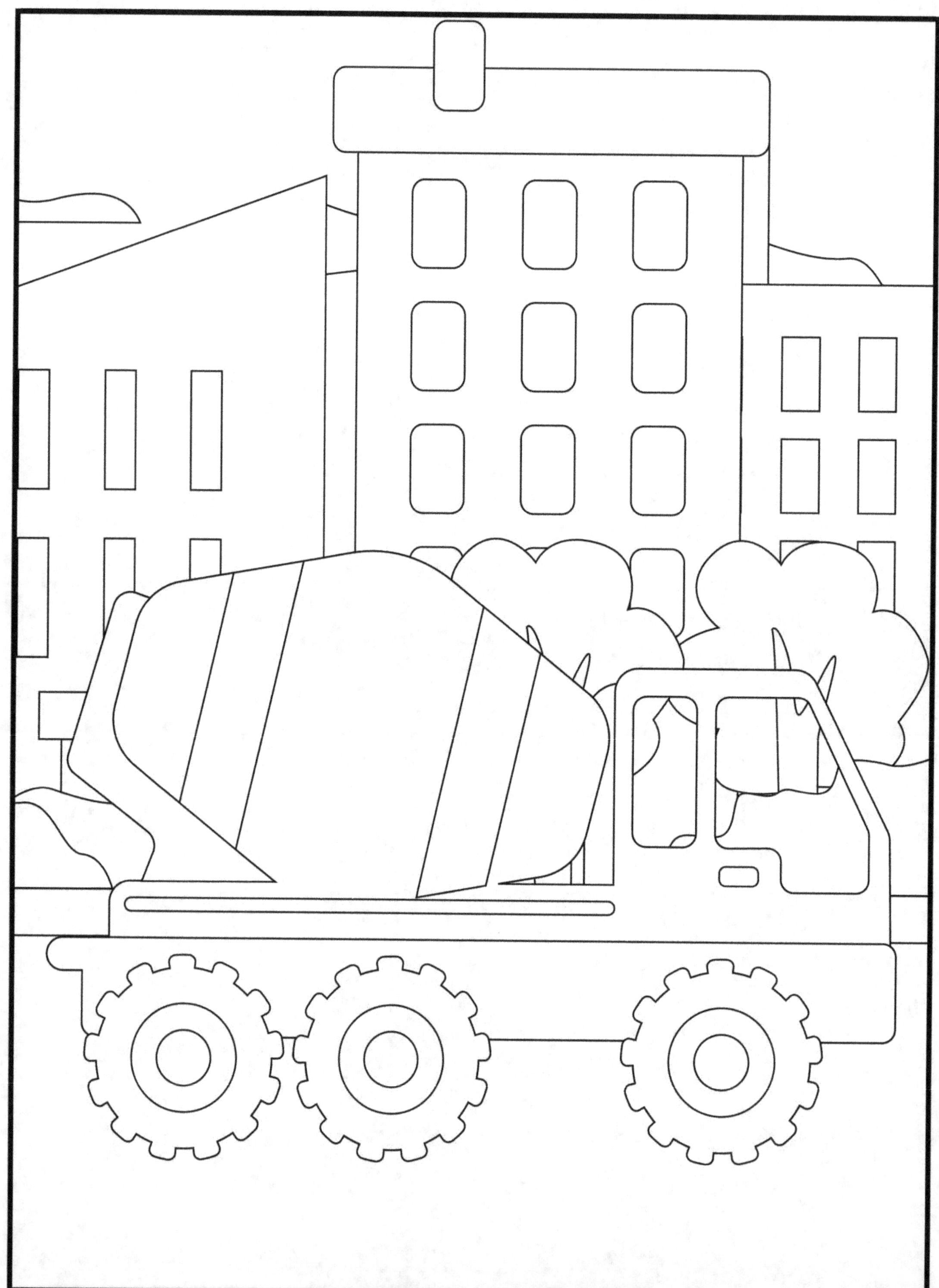

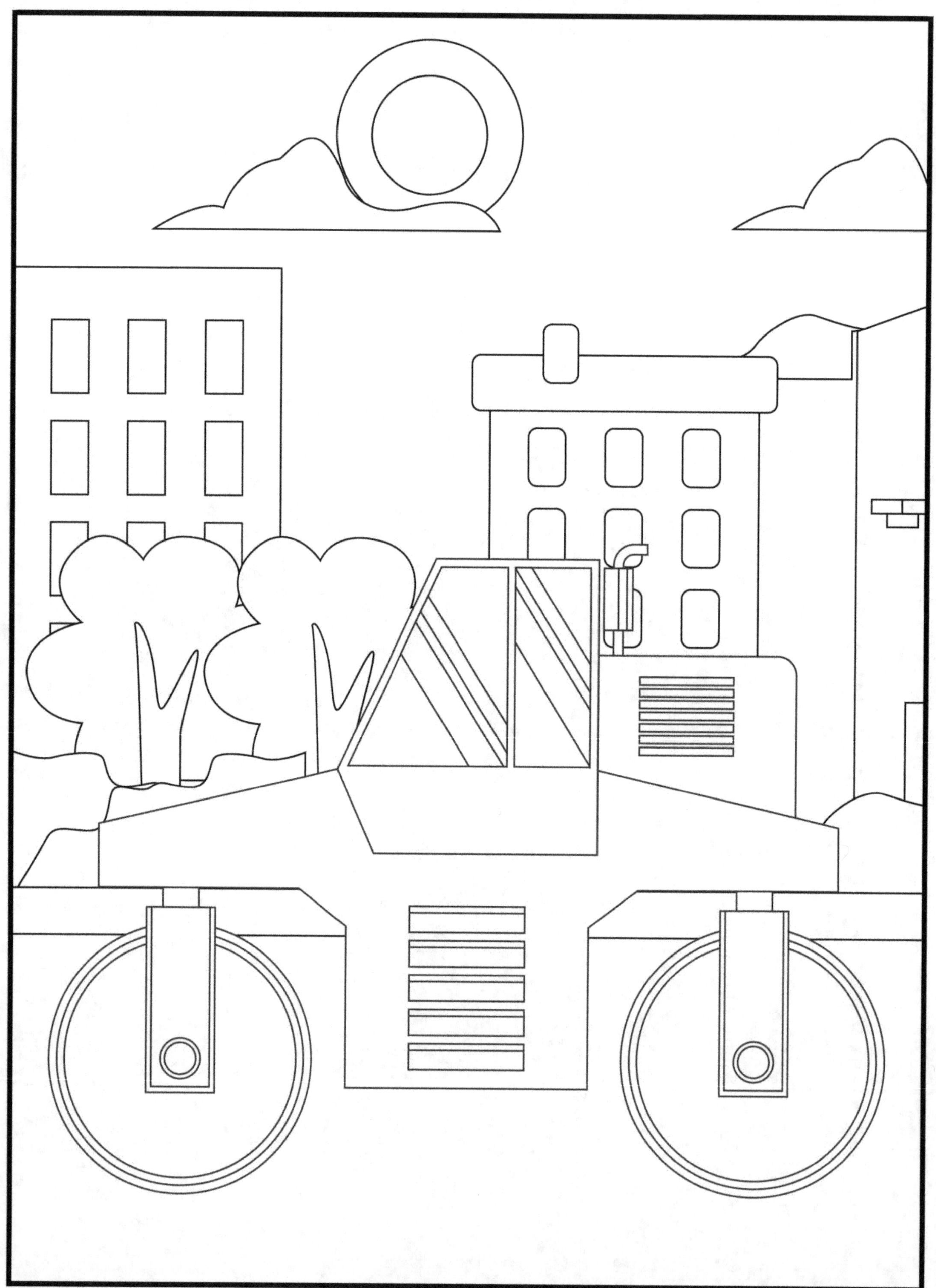

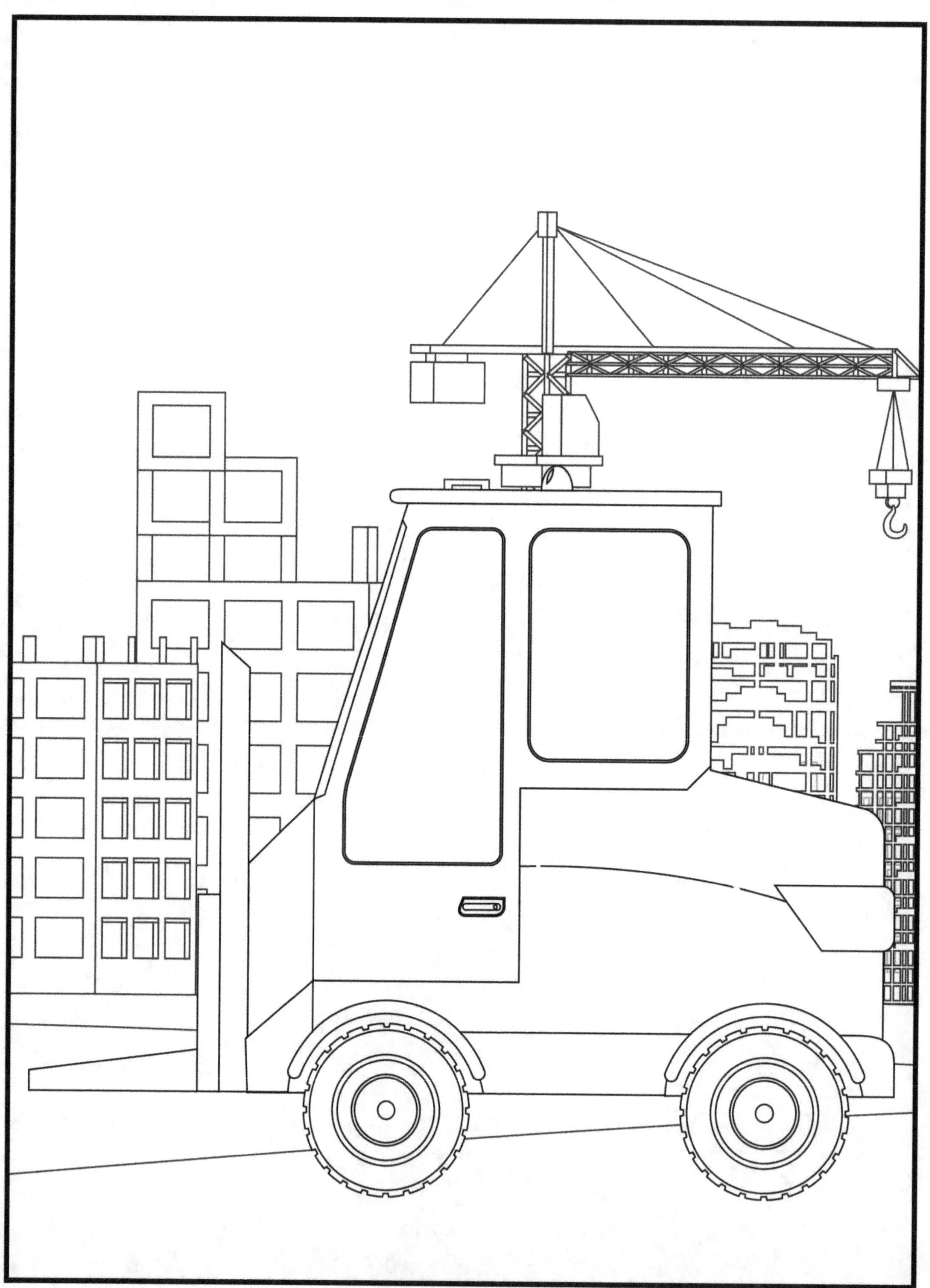

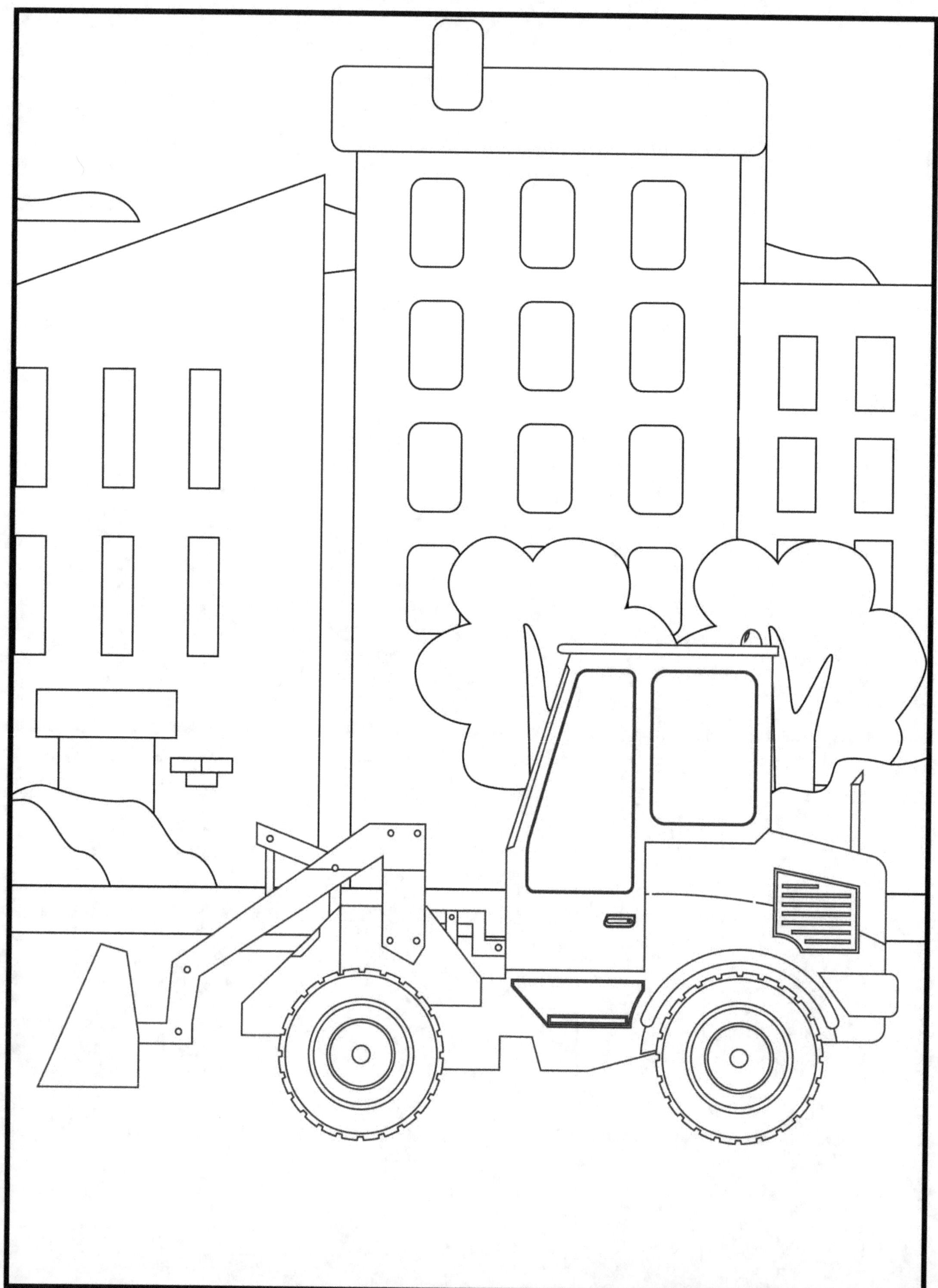

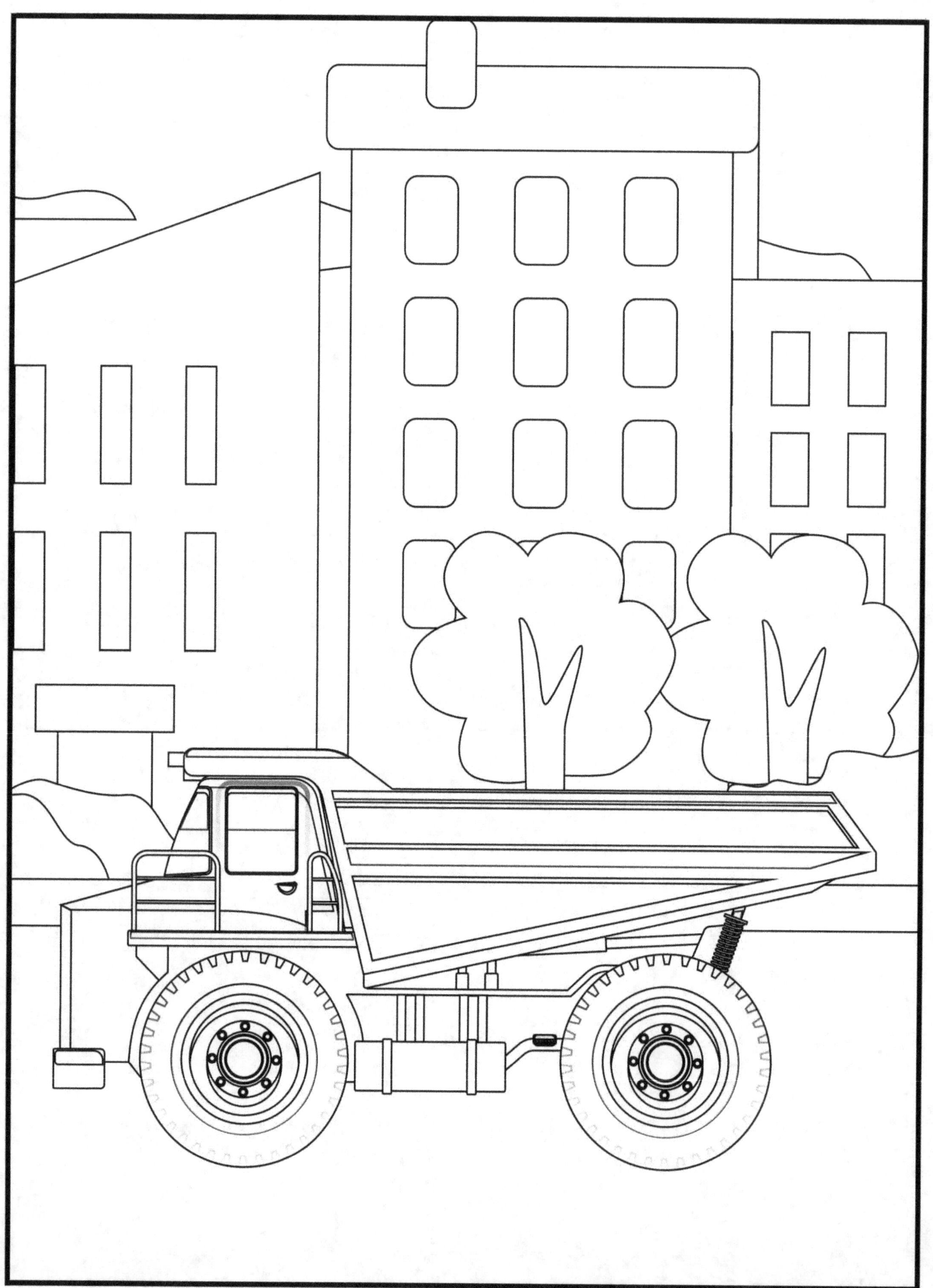

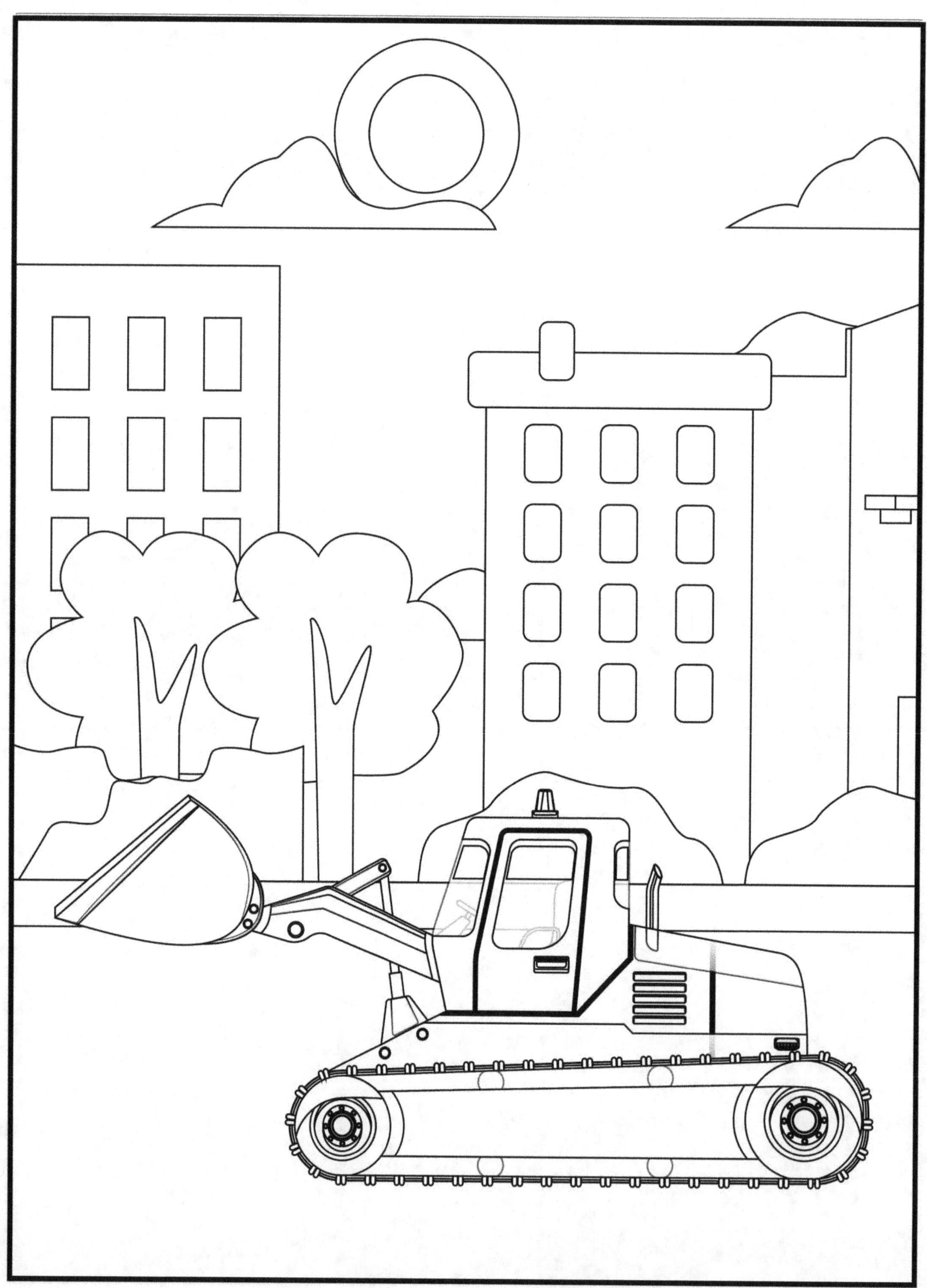

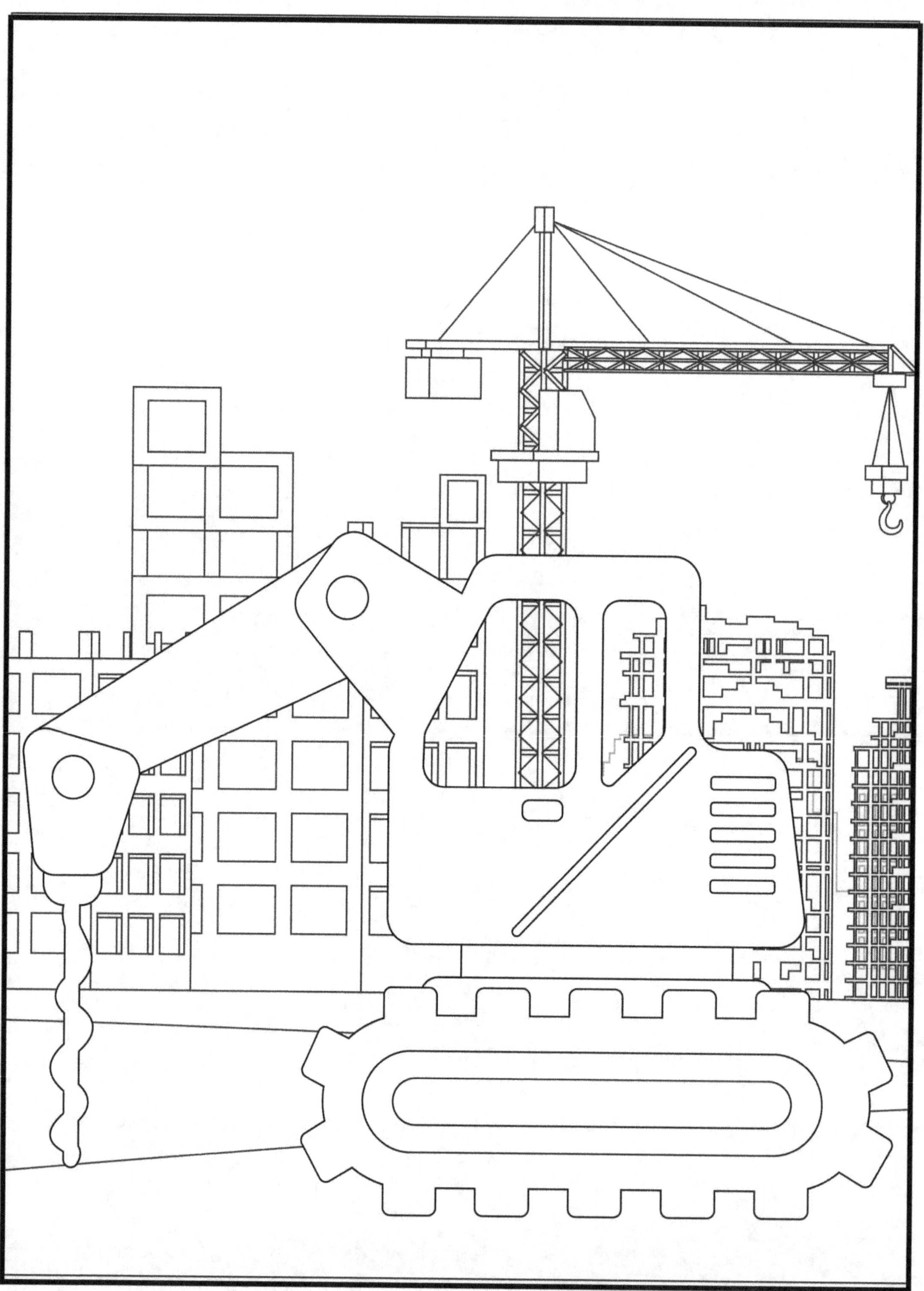

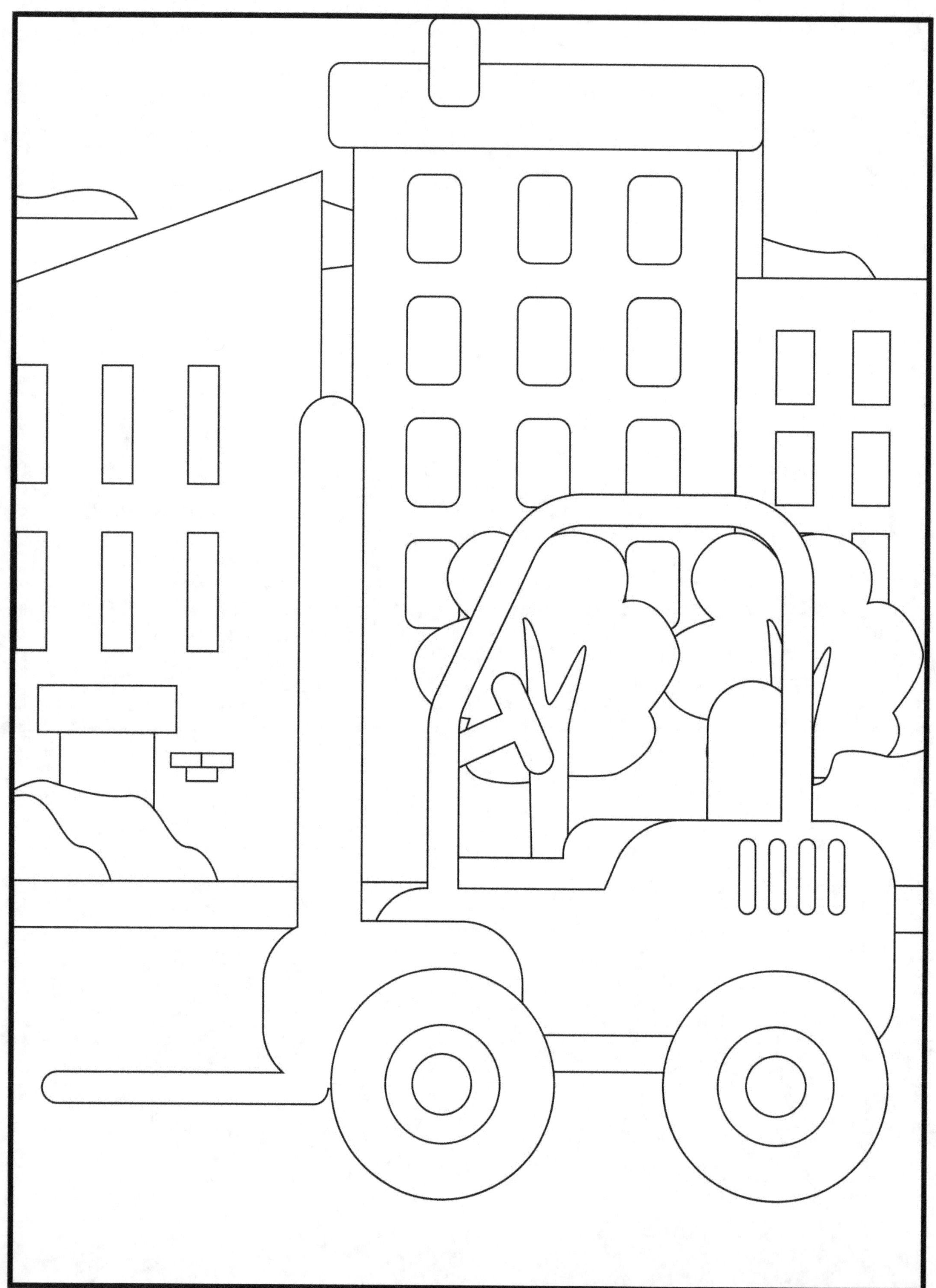

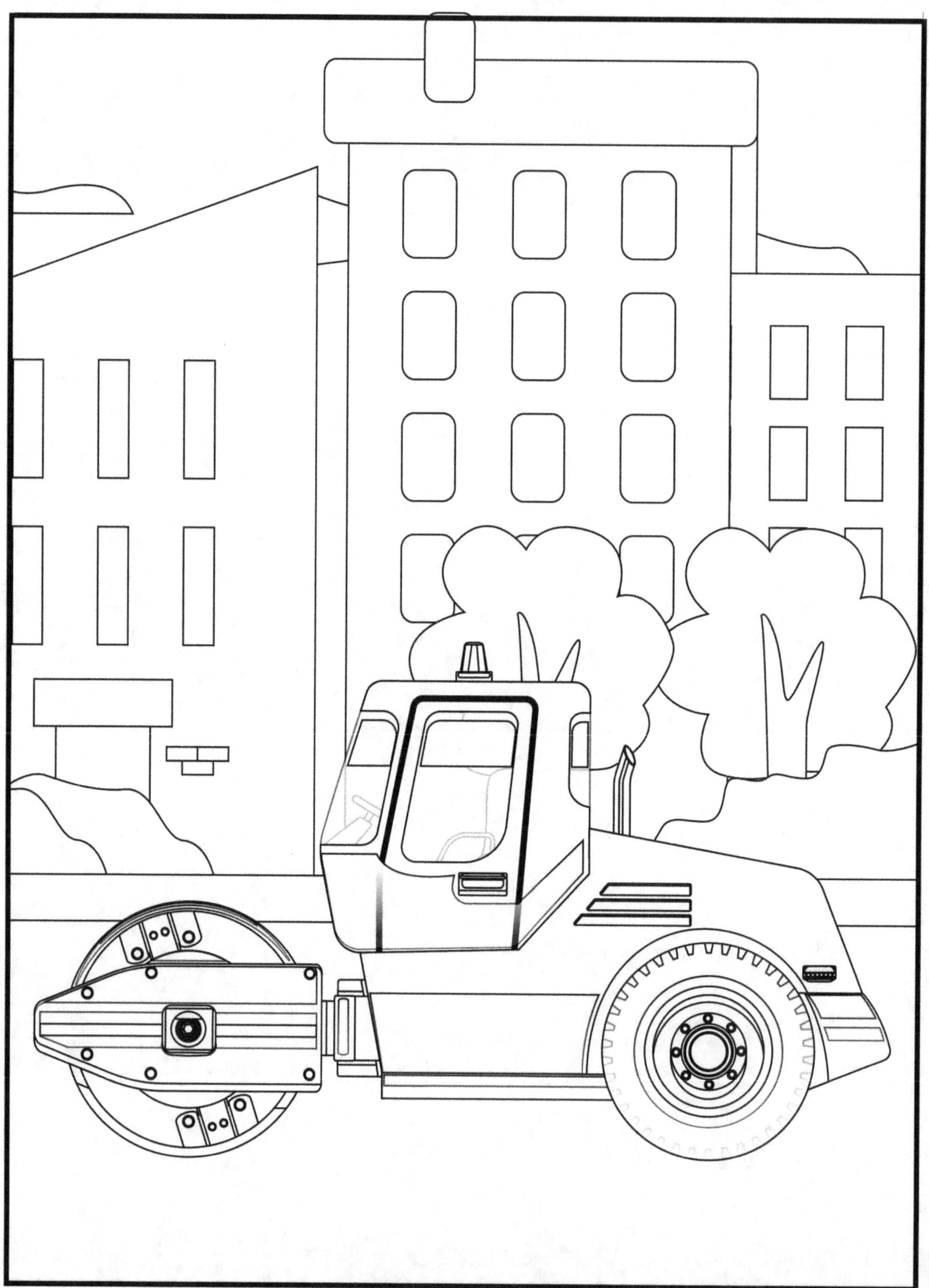

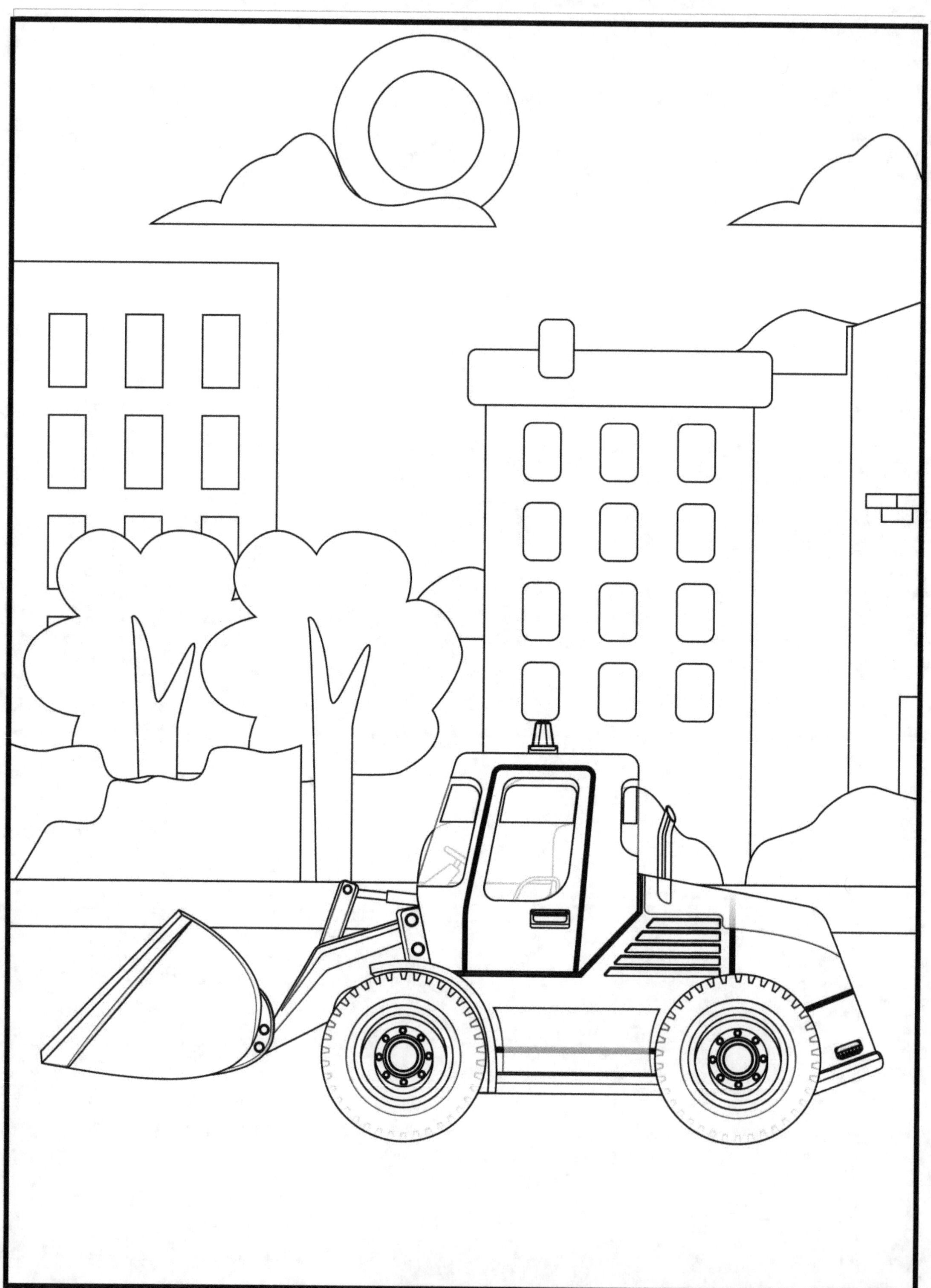

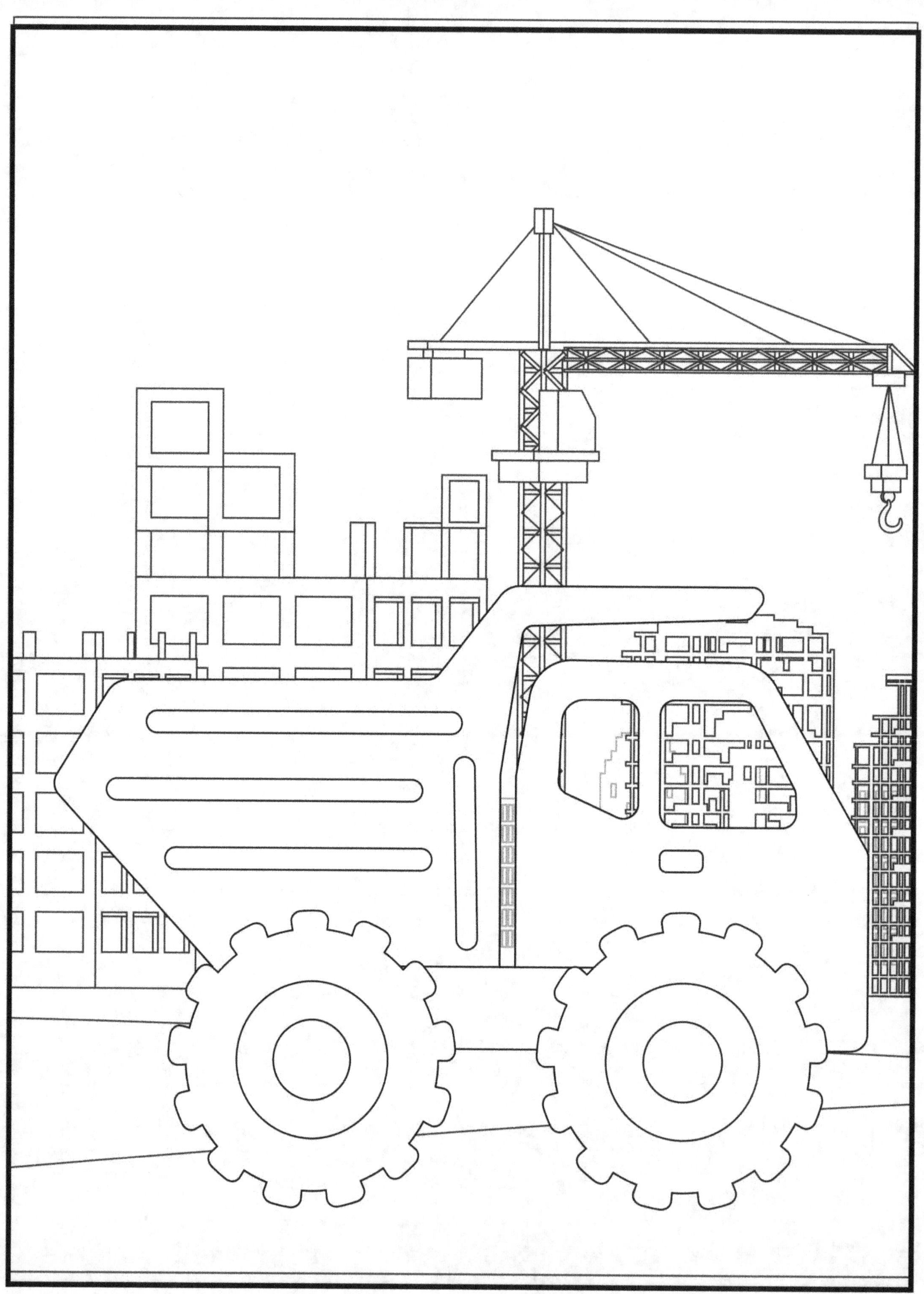

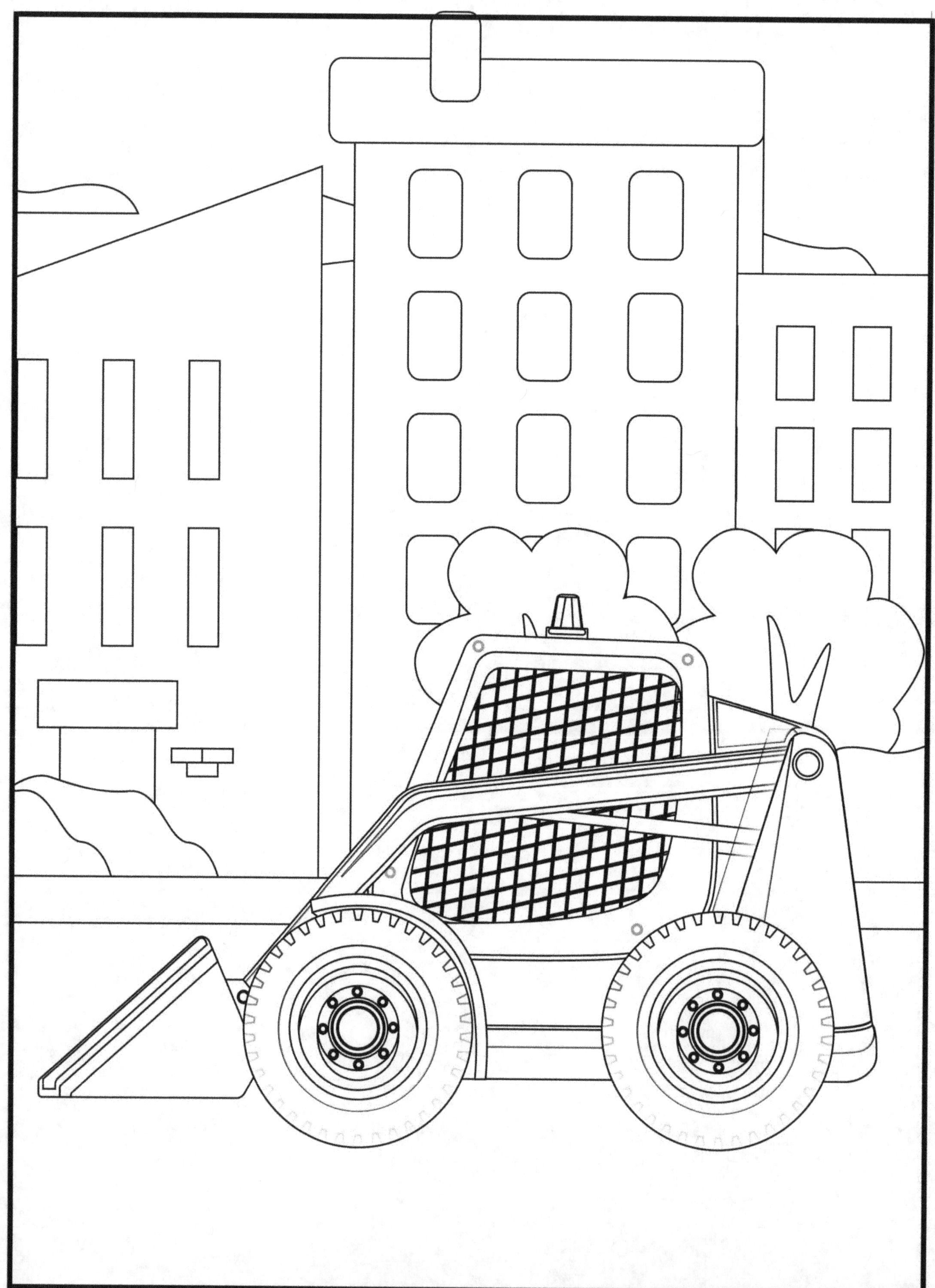

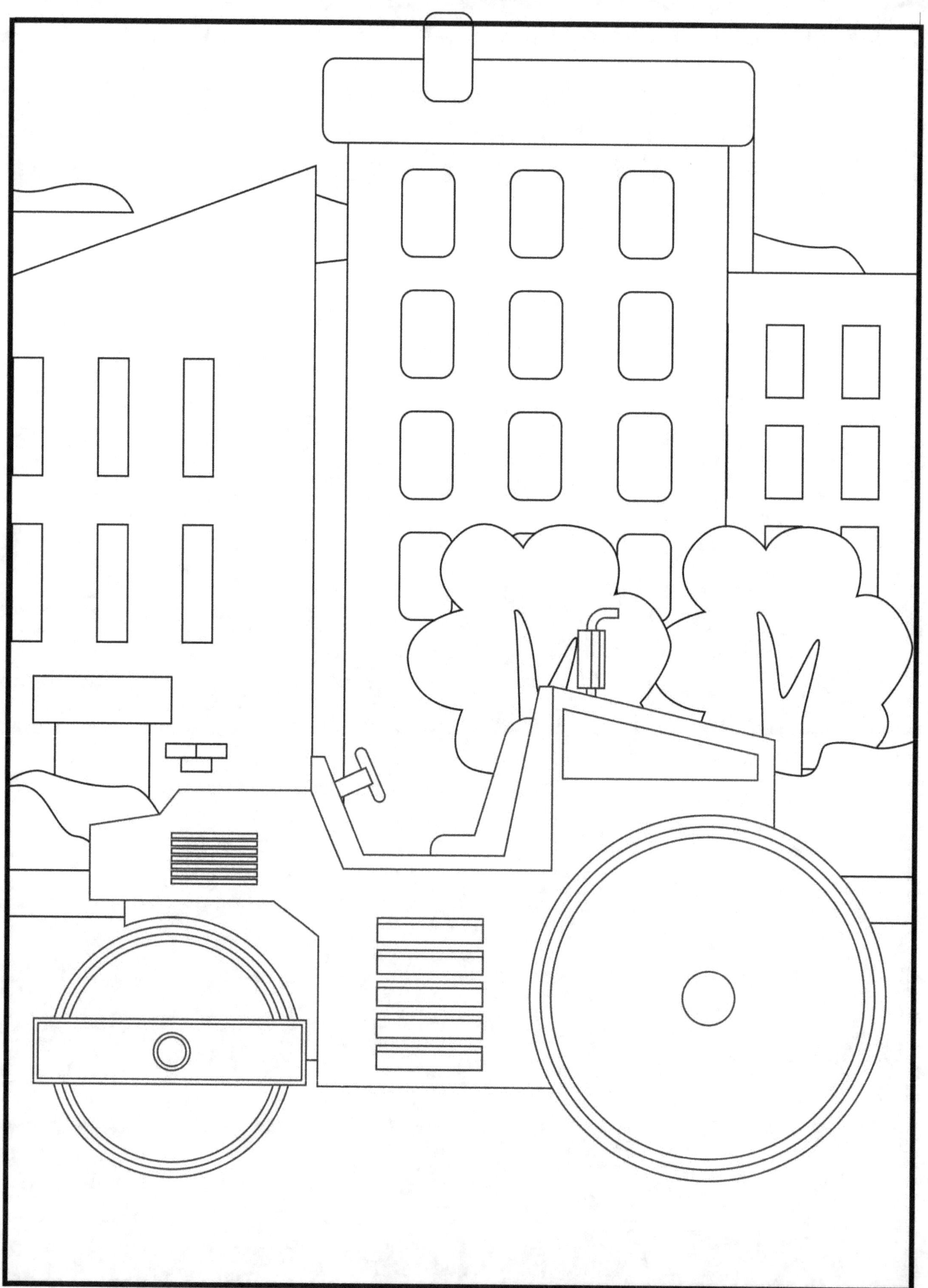

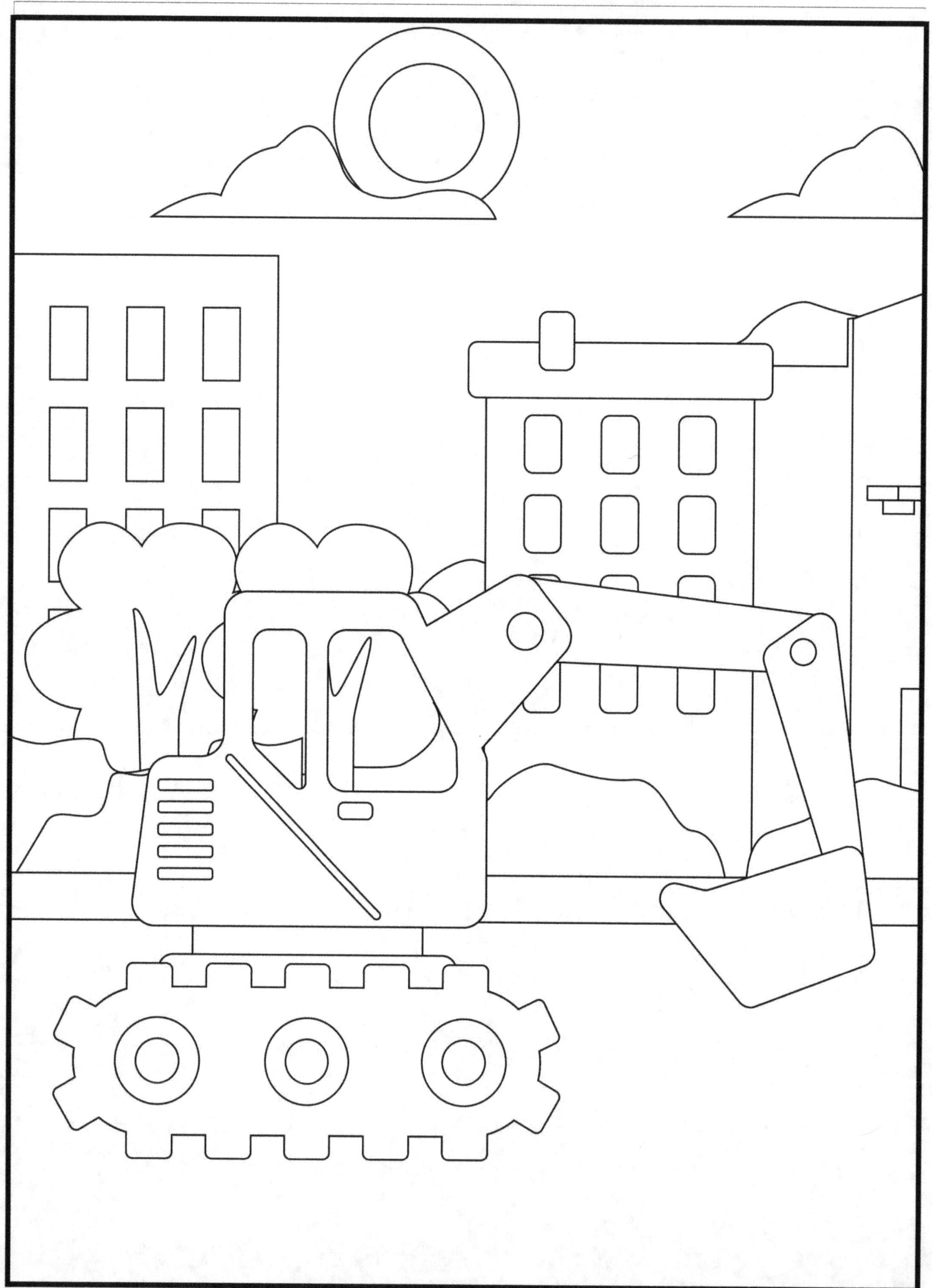

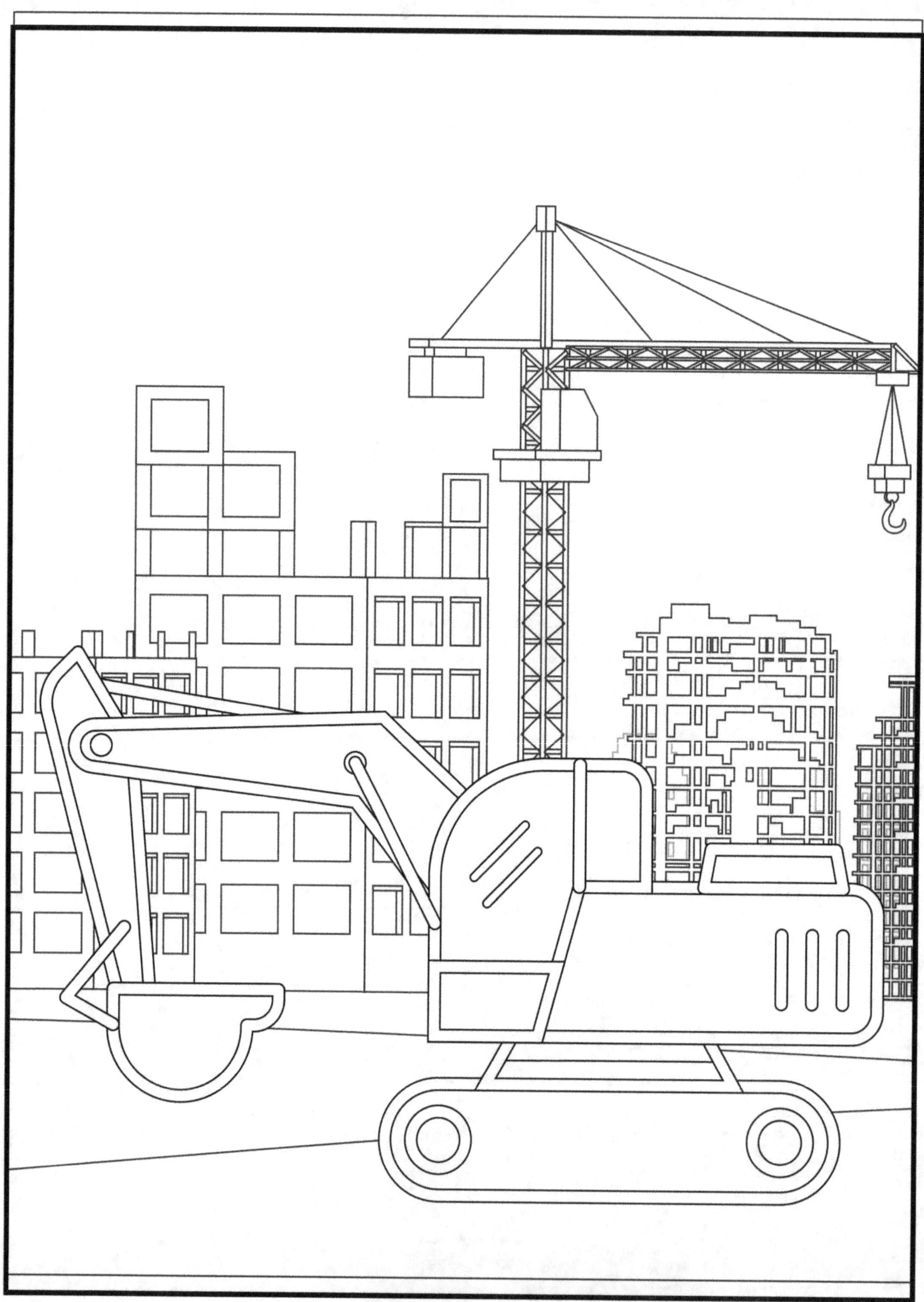

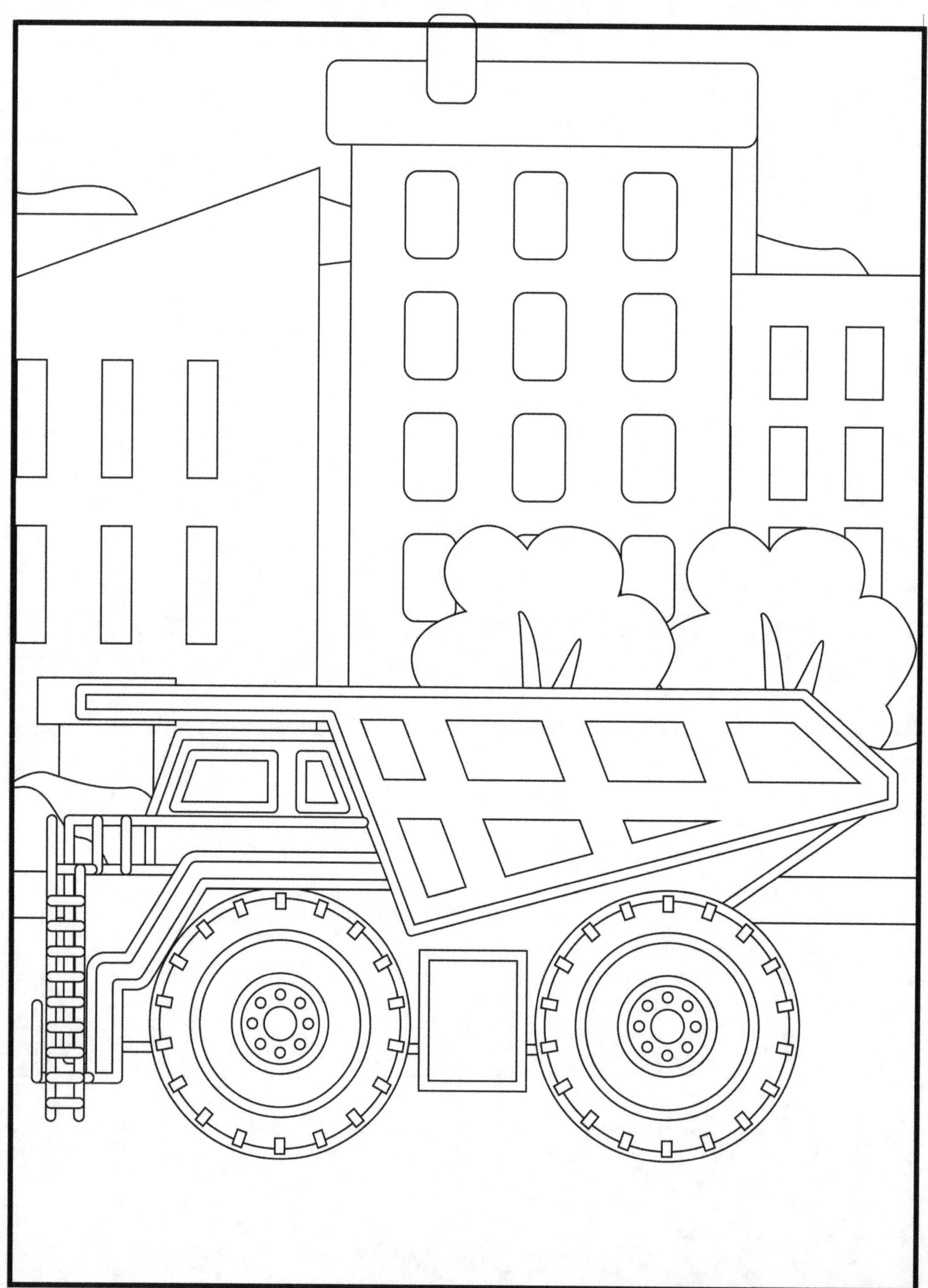

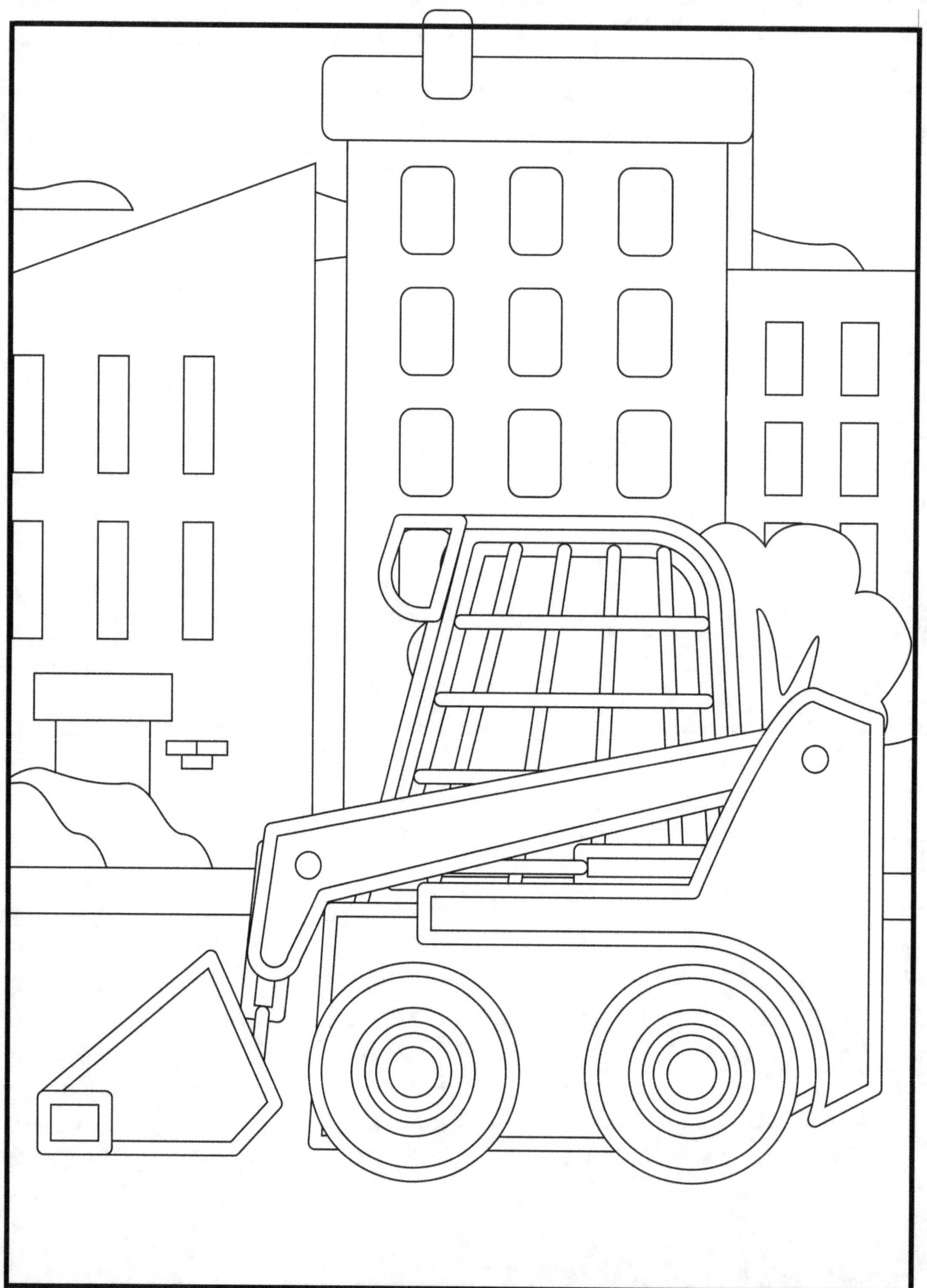

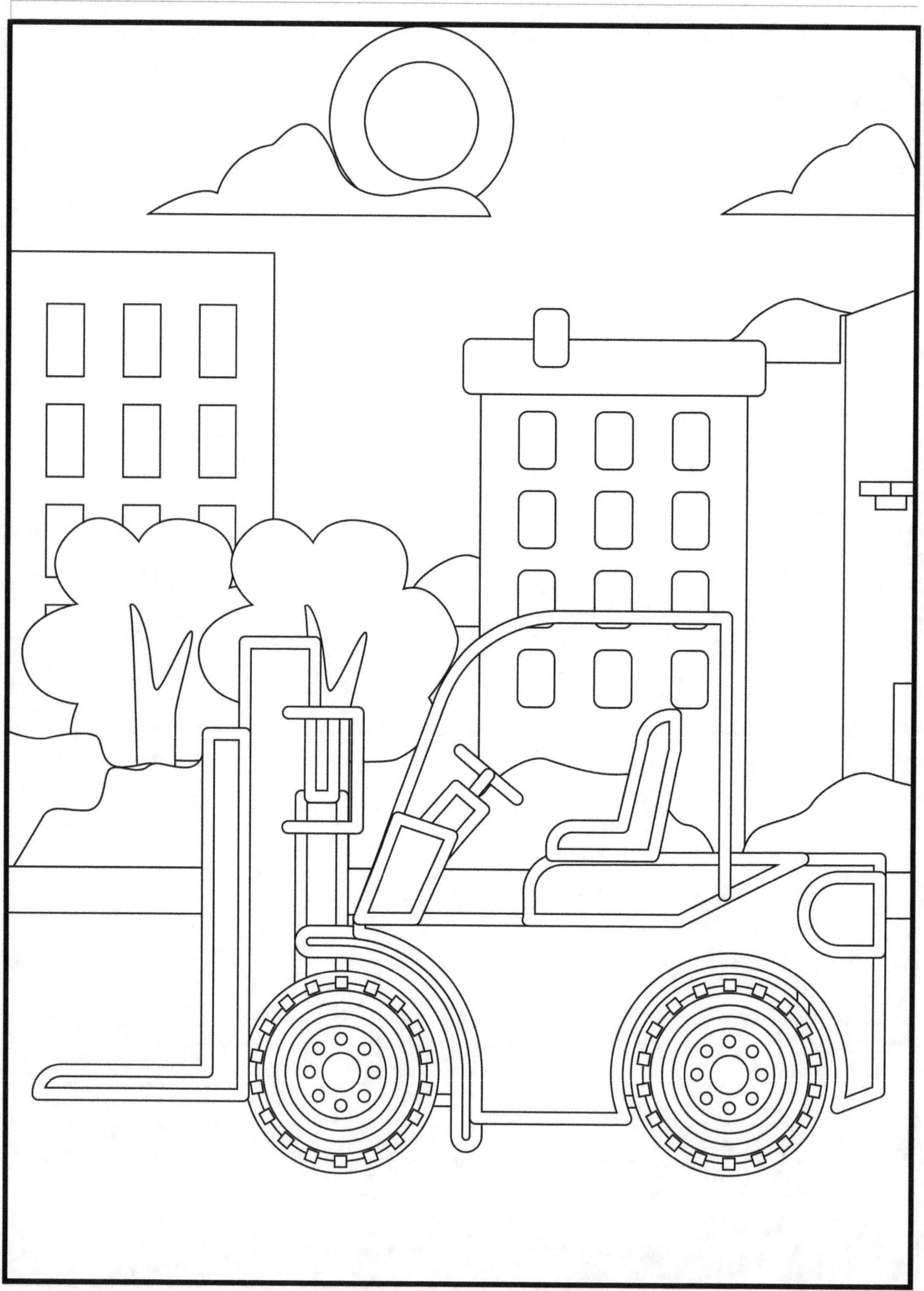

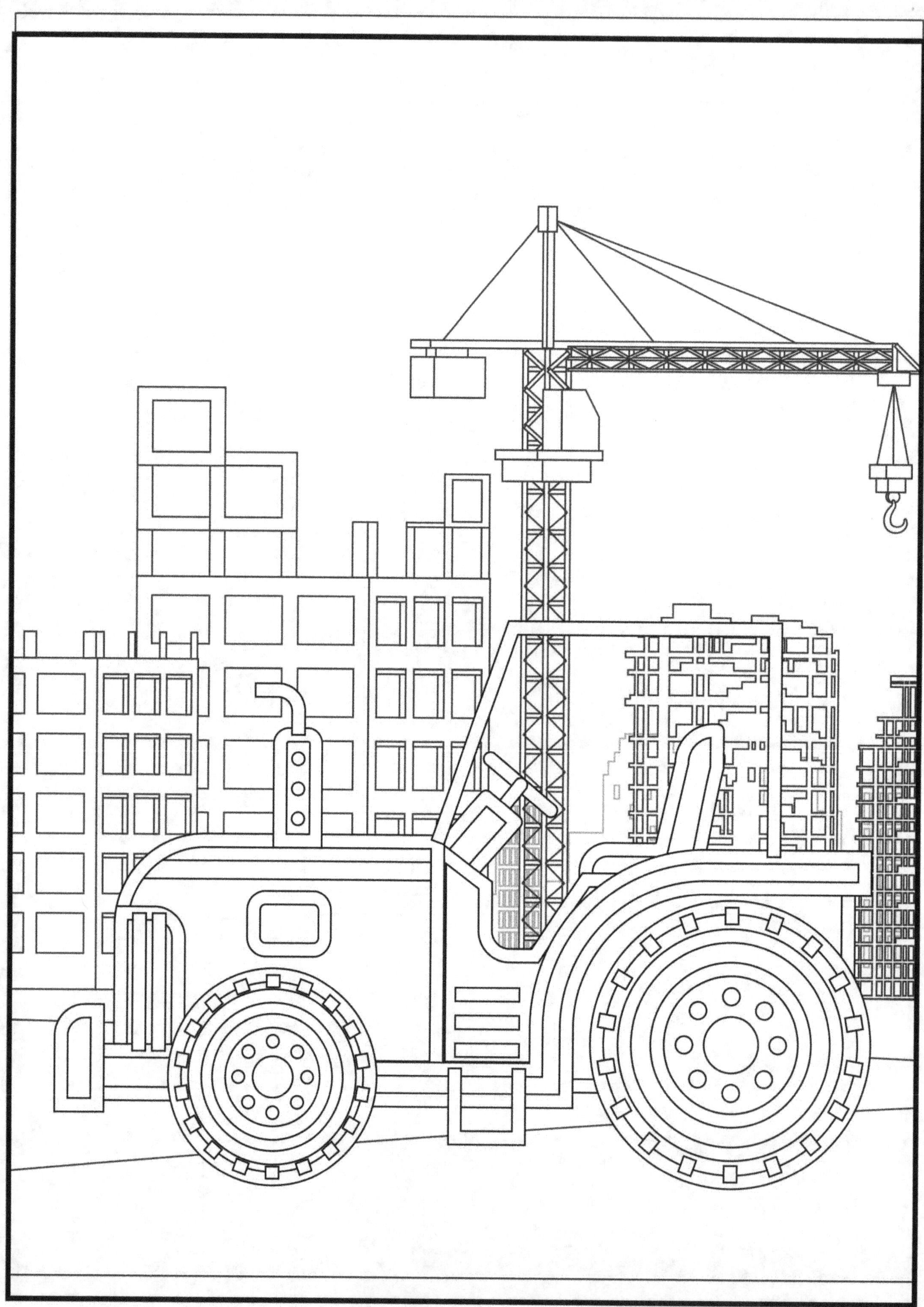

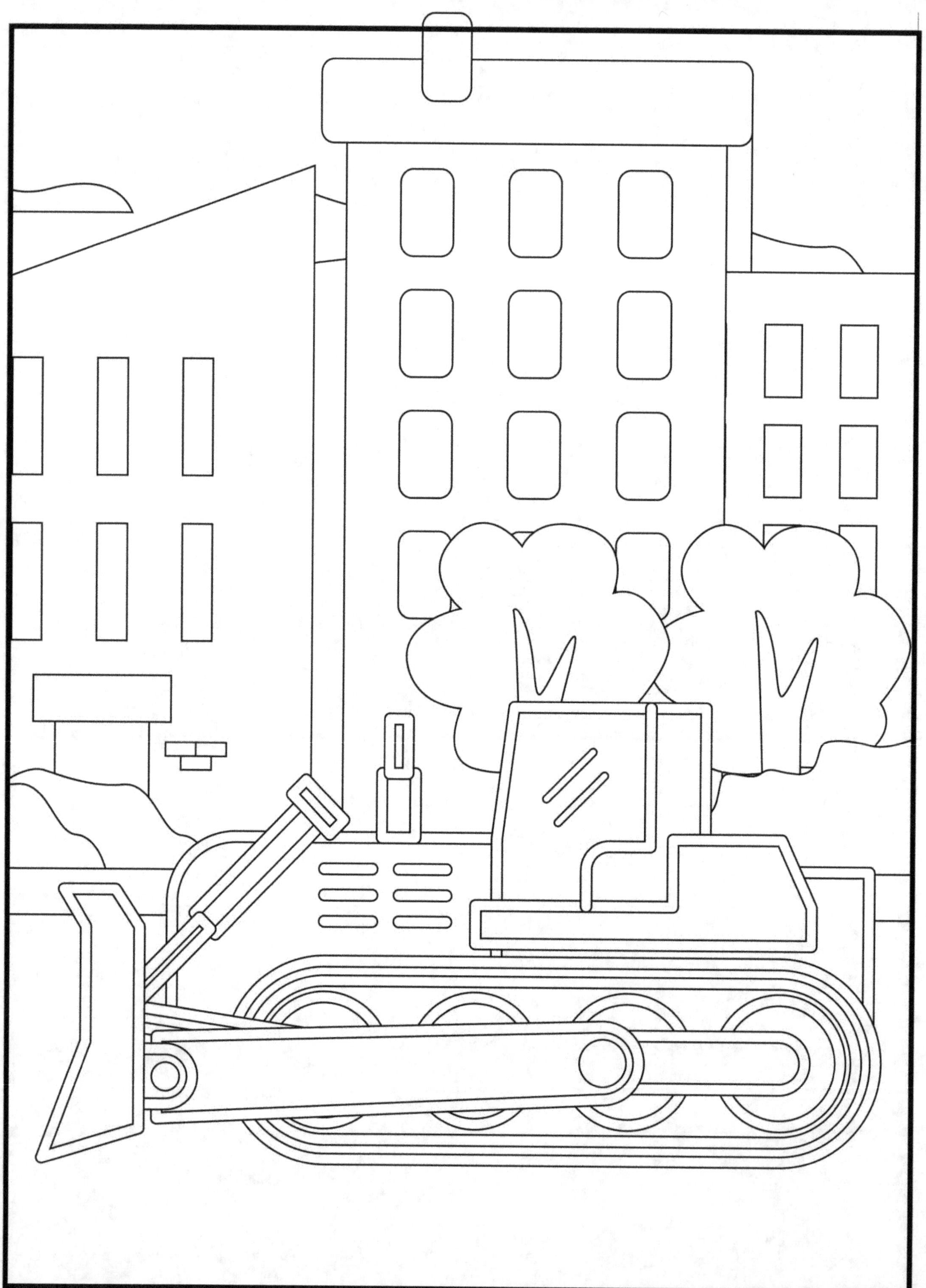

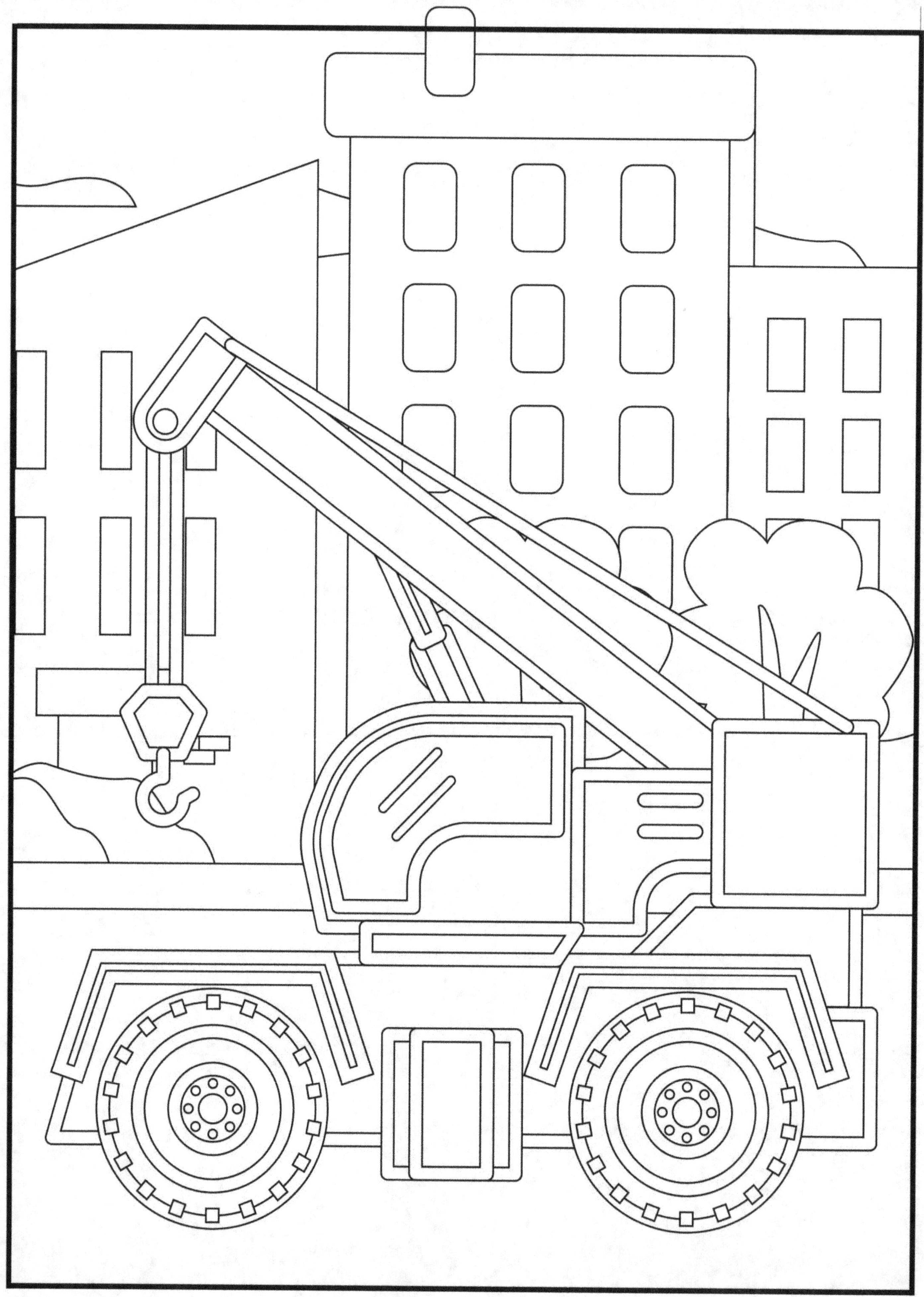

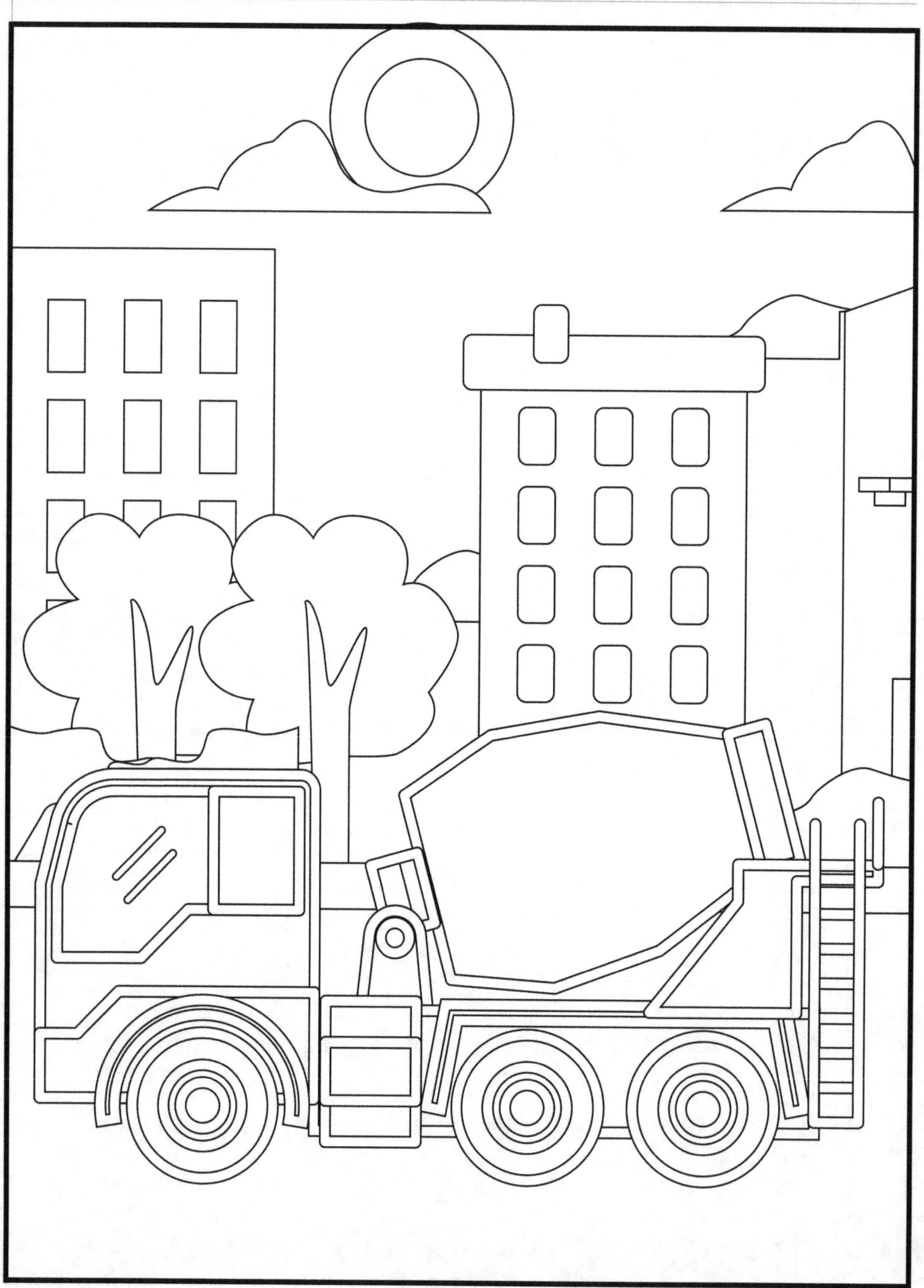

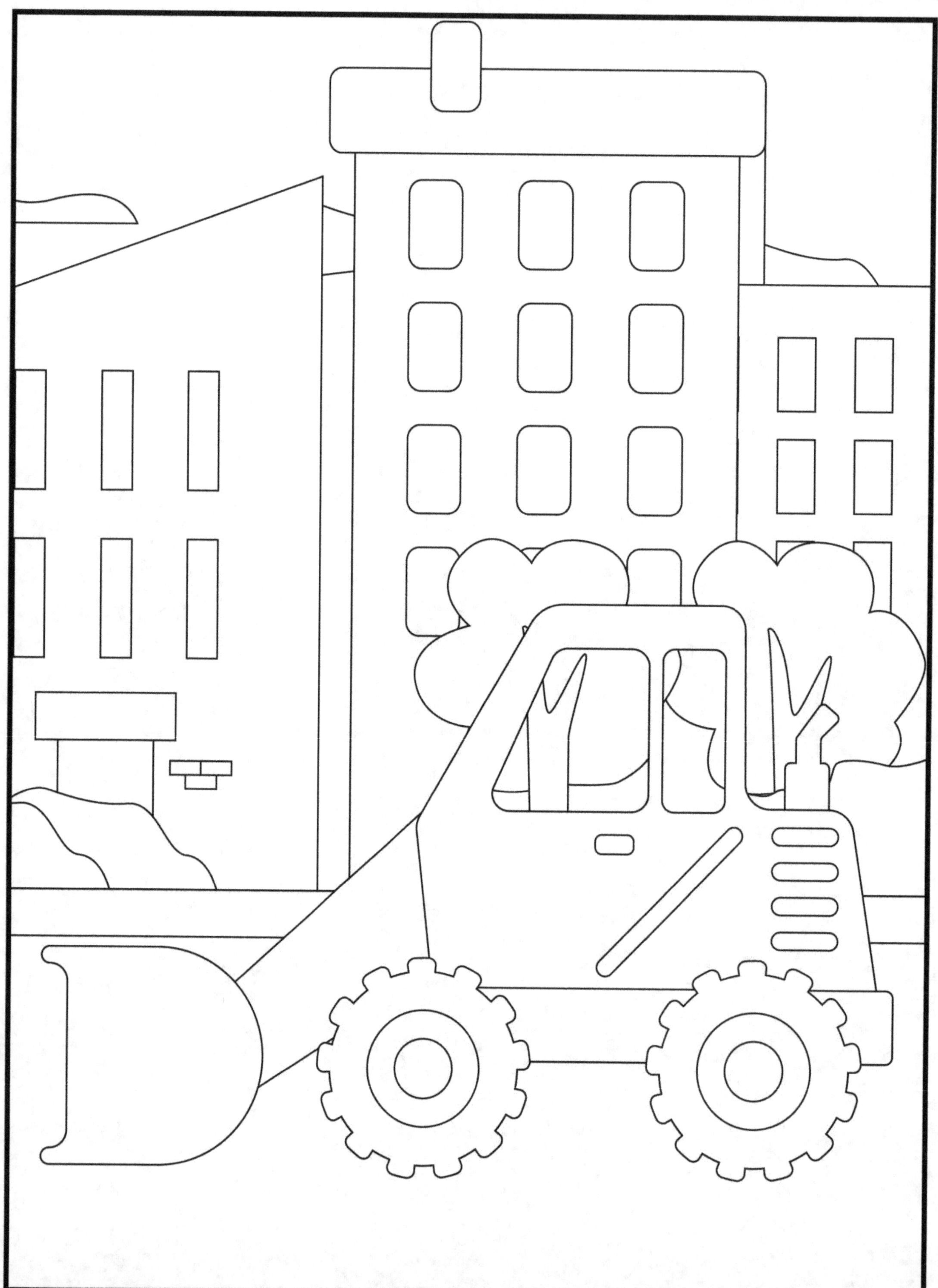

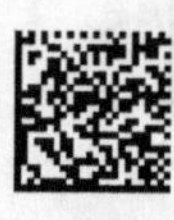